IT BEGINS WITH
I Do

IT BEGINS WITH
I Do

Happily Married Doesn't
Just Happen

ESTRELLA CUDMORE, CPC
AND ROBERT CUDMORE

ACKNOWLEDGEMENTS

The authors would like to express their appreciation to all that made this book possible. We especially want to thank those that provided valuable feedback on the manuscript.

It Begins with I Do

Front cover photograph by Crystal Shaw via Unsplash
Entwined rings design by Danny Johnson/Articulate Design

Loran Coaching
13359 N. Hwy 183, Ste 406 #178
Austin, TX 78750

ISBN: 978-1-7373333-0-2

For our amazing sons, Dorian and Alec,

and their bright futures.

Love does not consist of gazing at each other, but in looking outward together in the same direction.
- Antoine de Saint-Exupéry

CONTENTS

NOTE FROM THE AUTHORS

There are hundreds of books about marriage on the market. What makes this book different than most is that it was written by a married couple working side by side, writing about their own experiences in the adventure of marriage. In fact, this book could only be written by a married couple if it were to keep the tone, content, and character that it has. We're not saying that a book on marriage written by Joe Shmoe PhD doesn't have value, but it will almost certainly view marriage from a clinical perspective, rather than from an insider's view with insights from both halves of the marital equation, written by a couple who has spent decades working with young couples as they prepare for married life.

That said, this book was written by two people with very different personalities, and you will likely hear the two *voices* in the writing. Robert is highly analytical, logical, and process-oriented, while also possessing a dry, sarcastic, sometimes childish wit. Meanwhile, Estrella is more intuitive, sensing, nurturing, and possesses significantly higher emotional intelligence. This is one reason the book was long in the undertaking, since those two perspectives sometimes came from very different directions on any one topic, and it took time to shape each sentence, paragraph, and chapter to accommodate them both. That sounds a lot like marriage: two distinct persons with different perspectives working at one common goal.

It took us more than fifteen years to write this book, not because it's a particularly long book, but simply because life kept getting in the way. However, we returned to the endeavor over and over through the years, determined to get our message out that happy marriage does exist and can be had. We continued to put new learnings into the book as we went.

Because the writing spanned most of two decades, the world has changed some in those intervening years. What constitutes wholesomeness has continued to change, and the institution of marriage and marital roles is often mocked and ridiculed like never before. However, our own view of what a successful relationship looks like remains unchanged since we shared vows more than three decades ago, and we firmly believe that this view is one of the keys to the continued success and happiness of our marriage.

There is no book on earth that can fix an already broken marriage; only extensive counseling from a good marriage counselor has a chance of bringing that situation back from the brink. But a book – this book – might be just the thing to help a relationship that is struggling a bit and just needs some fresh ideas to overcome obstacles, or address specific areas of concern, or breathe some new life into the couple's routines.

It is said that one should "write about what you know," so that is exactly what we've done here. This book presents a glimpse into how we've maintained a successful, happy marriage for more than three decades. We know many happy couples, so we are well aware that ours is not the only happy marriage, and ours is not the only path to get there, nor the only model for what happy marriage looks like. But this is *our* book, so we are sharing *our* methods in the hope that we can help couples who may need it, and perhaps provide a little entertainment for couples who don't.

When asked why we chose to write this book, the answer is simple: we want to grow the number of happily married couples in this world. It is the same reason we coach engaged couples year after year to help them start marriage on the right foot. If this book reaches just one couple who we can't personally work with, helping them move from married to happily-married – or from unmarried to happily-married – it was well worth the effort.

We don't believe we've included any content that is considered especially controversial, but our focus is on marriage rather than political correctness, so you'll have to decide that for yourself. We feel that most couples will get something from this book, regardless of how much their values or background may differ from ours. If that doesn't happen, you might want to look for that book by Joe Shmoe PhD. But it is our hope that at least some of the concepts and stories in our book will make your marriage stronger, refreshed, and more enjoyable, and hopefully provide a laugh or two.

- Estrella & Robert Cudmore, Austin, Texas, 2021

/

Coming together is the beginning.
Keeping together is progress. Working
together is success.
- Henry Ford

1

You Made It Through the Wedding. Now What?

Jack and Jill went up the hill, not to fetch a pail of water, but to be joined forever in holy matrimony. Why shouldn't they? They're mature adults. They love each other. They dated for the requisite two years, followed by a proper twelve-month engagement. Everyone thinks they make a great couple.

Like most girls, Jill has dreamed about this day for most of her life. By age fourteen, she had a complete fantasy assembled in her head. She has pictured the dress, the church, the perfect flowers, the music selection, and bridesmaid's colors. The identity of the groom is the last piece of the puzzle, although she knows what his tuxedo will look like. She doesn't know precisely what he looks like, but she is sure that he will sweep her off her feet and bound away with her to a castle far, far away.

Meanwhile, Jack spent his childhood like most boys, dreaming about the day he'd join the Major League and spend his days traveling from city to city playing the All-American game. He spent hours arguing the virtues of wearing shorts rather than pants to church on Sunday, because wearing pants equates to getting dressed up. The only time he thinks of weddings is when he is developing schemes to use on his parents to get out of having to attend one. As far as wedding fantasy goes, his fantasy is limited to the wedding night when all the hoopla is over, and the *real* fun begins, though he is not completely sure what that means. And, is there such thing as tuxedo shorts?

These differences between the male and female of our species are yet another example of God's infinite sense of humor. How the female ever succeeds in finding and marrying a mate is nothing short of a miracle. However, every weekend in places of worship, gardens, and courthouses around the world, couples find themselves in front of clergy, judges, or even ships' captains to make this phenomenal commitment to love, honor, and cherish until death do them part. From there the story should read "and they lived happily ever after." Why is it this so seldom comes true?

The high divorce rate is the most obvious indicator that happily ever after often fails. But this isn't the whole story. What about all those couples who avoid divorce, only to spend a lifetime together without wedded bliss? It ranges from a quiet, cold, indifferent coexistence to all-out war, yet the couple may stay together for reasons *they* may not even understand. If the divorce rate hovers around 50%, and some amount of the 50% that remain married are *un*happily married, how small is the pool of happily married people?

With so much marital strife in the world, it's hard to spot that small segment of the married population that manages to hold onto those marital ideals – those same ideals which most of us comprehend *prior* to the leap into marriage – and to enjoy married life. Many people may dismiss this minority group as abnormal, a lark, or even a myth. "I heard they spotted a happily married couple down by the canyon this morning, but it just turned out to be Bigfoot." They'll say that those happily married couples simply got lucky in somehow finding their soulmate; it was the alignment of the stars, or any number of other coincidences. But does it really come down to just being lucky, or is there something these successful, content couples do – or don't do – that is different from the rest?

For that matter, what are soulmates, if not simply two people who love each other while also having a propensity for extending affection, consideration, respect, courtesy, loyalty, kindness, and selflessness to the other person? In a mature relationship this reveals itself in a couple that still thoroughly enjoys spending time together after decades of marriage, never running out of things to talk about or new adventures to share. Therefore, assuming two people truly love one another, if the soulmates experience is about attitudes and behaviors, can a couple *become* soulmates by changing how they interact with each other until habits are formed?

Marriage is more than just the flowing white dress, the flowers, the music, and the size of the bar tab on the big day. The wedding ceremony is just the champagne bottle bursting on the hull of a new ship about to set sail. The ship must be seaworthy and the crew competent to complete the voyage and arrive at the destination. Marriage can be a ship of fools, the ill-fated Titanic, or it can be a pleasure cruise. But that last result isn't achieved without effort.

Choices we make from the very beginning – or even before the beginning – mold the relationship. It is said that a new couple's behavior in the first six months of marriage sets the stage for their behavior for the remainder of the marriage. The new groom that is more interested in spending afternoons and weekends on the golf course during those first few months is more likely to find, years later, that his wife wants to take a relaxing cruise with her girlfriends – no husbands allowed – a little too often. The wife that constantly nags during those first months may wonder how it came to be that her husband suffers spontaneous deafness whenever she is speaking to him, but can somehow hear the sports scores on the evening news coming from the house next door.

Our behavior and choices mold the relationship.

On the surface, it seems that marriages are either doomed to failure, or destined for success. In truth, no marriage has its course set in advance. Good marriages are mostly the result of mutual respect, careful planning, and a stream of sound choices. Good marriages are about sacrifice and compromise, and although these words can sometimes evoke negative connotations, they are instrumental in developing a healthy relationship. These efforts, behaviors, and attitudes don't stop after the first few months or few years. They must continue until death do you part.

For the first several years of our own marriage, we assumed that most marriages were like ours; that is, living happily ever after. But as time went by, and we had the opportunity to know and observe more couples, we realized that we were one of those *abnormal* marriages. Other couples tell us that we're weird because we actually like each other, and they say we aren't supposed to be so happy after so many years of marriage. Love is supposed to fade away, they tell us. We were once mistaken for a new couple still in the dating process because we were "so civilized with one another," but we had already been married for twenty years at that time. It made us wonder what we were doing differently from these other couples.

It's easy to chalk it up to us just being soulmates who happened to find each other, but according to the Myers-Briggs personality test we took as part of our marriage preparation, we were starting on shaky ground. We were polar opposites in so many ways from a personality perspective, and our backgrounds – culturally, socioeconomically, and spiritually – provided almost no common-ground for compatibility. It was our choices and actions made as a married couple, rather than who we were when we first met, that shaped how our relationship evolved as a couple. That effort continues to this day.

Could we share the subconscious system that has made our marriage happy for over thirty years? This book is our effort to document our techniques, routines, and successes, providing real life examples from our journey through marriage, and from our observations of other couples (names have been changed to protect the innocent, and not so innocent). We hope that our story might give helpful tips to new couples just starting out and help rekindle the fire for those mature couples that may be struggling and not know why. Though any wife or husband can benefit from the topics discussed herein, it is the couple that reads this book together that will achieve the best results. It takes two to tango.

Many people spend more time in
planning the wedding than they do in
planning the marriage.
- Zig Ziglar

2

The Business of Marriage

What company opens its doors for the first time without appropriate planning? The answer: one that is doomed to failure. For a business to have a chance at success, it needs to have several things in place before the doors open for the first time, including a strong business plan that is agreed to by all parties, dedicated and motivated partners who know one another well and have a high degree of trust, and at least the minimum of assets.

Once the company is up and running, the partners need only refer to the business plan to ensure roles and responsibilities are being followed, meaningful performance goals are in place and being met, and the right products or services are being produced in the right quantities and at the right time. A quarterly review of the finances determines whether or not financial and operational goals are being met, and what, if any, changes need to be made for the upcoming quarter. A yearly review of the business and business plan allows the partners to make the *tweaks* necessary to keep the business on the right track, or it may even be time for the business plan itself to be modified and updated.

Exclusive of the love and emotional attachments, which are unique and important components of a lasting intimate relationship, marriage can look a lot like a business. A partnership is formed, a contract is signed, including all the requisite terms and conditions, and the doors open for business. But wait. What about the business plan, the financial goals, the roles and responsibilities, and the products and services that you plan to offer? Too many couples get married without agreeing to these important elements and may never get around to working them out after the vows are taken, resulting in the cause of many marital problems.

Marriage and business can look a lot alike.

Disagreements regarding finances (Profit & Loss), which person will be responsible for what duties (Roles & Responsibilities), whether or not to have children, how many, and when (Products and release schedules), and how time and resources will be used (Operations) lead to the demise of many relationships. It's never too late for a partnership to become stronger, and to create a new business plan that has these important factors in place. Once done, don't forget to update that business plan through the years to account for changes such as an empty nest, aging parents, and retirement.

Know Your Business Partner

"Macadamia nuts roasting on an open fire, Robert Frost scribbling out his prose. A girl named Carol, being stung by a--"

"Karl, if you're going to sing Christmas songs, why can't you sing them correctly?" Kathy asks, smiling, as she hangs another ornament on the tree. "It's chestnuts, chestnuts!"

"But I don't like chestnuts. I prefer macadamia nuts," Karl replies in his usual deadpan humor.

A few minutes later, *"Christmas is coming, the barbeque ribs are getting fat--"*

"Karl!"

"Well, have you ever eaten a goose? I haven't either, but I'm pretty sure barbeque ribs are tastier," Karl says. "You know, these Christmas carols are making me hungry."

Meet Karl and Kathy. They've been married about ten years, and have two grade school-aged boys. Along with their sons, they are busy this Saturday morning with their annual tradition of putting up Christmas decorations, including decorating the tree with ornaments and lights, as they all drink hot chocolate. The smell of the Christmas tree fills the house, helping with the festive ambiance. Karl is also busy with his other annual tradition of massacring Christmas carols.

"Deck the malls with cows on trolleys, fa la la la--"

"I can't believe Christmas is just a few weeks away," Kathy says, in a not-so-subtle attempt to move Karl off the carols. "It's going to be a little different from previous years now that your parents have moved back into town. Remind me, how long had it been since they moved away?"

"They moved away just a couple years before we got married.

In fact, I had just gotten back from helping with their move shortly before you and I met," Karl says.

After some contemplation, Kathy asks, "Do you think we'll all fit okay at the dining room table on Christmas Eve?"

"What do you mean?"

"Well, do you think we need to put the other leaf in the table to make more room, or can we just squeeze in the way it is?"

"My parents' table is plenty big enough for all of us," Karl replies.

"Why on earth would we borrow your parents' table when we can just add a leaf to ours?" Kathy asks.

"We're not borrowing their table. We're going to their house on Christmas Eve," Karl clarifies.

"Karl, stop goofing around," Kathy says, gently slapping his arm.

"I'm not goofing around. Didn't I tell you about this when my parents first moved back into town?"

"That was eight months ago, why would we have been discussing Christmas?" Kathy responds sharply, decorating coming to an abrupt halt.

"I thought I told you that when I was growing up it was tradition to spend Christmas Eve at the grandparents' house. I want the same thing for our kids. If your parents lived in town, we'd be going there, or taking turns if both sets of parents lived in town," Karl says evenly.

"I remember you mentioning going to your grandparent's house for Christmas when you were little, but I don't recall you mentioning that it was now *our* tradition," Kathy says. "I enjoy our Christmas Eve here at home. We've been doing it this way since we got married. We've always spent Easter with your parents, Thanksgiving with mine, and Christmas Eve here at home."

"Kathy, wouldn't you like to have our own children bringing their children to our house on Christmas Eve when we're the grandparents? I'm talking about carrying on family traditions. Is that wrong? As you pointed out, we go and stay with your parents every Thanksgiving. That's a tradition."

"Yes, but what about our own traditions? The ones you and I have been establishing since the day we got married?" Kathy asks. "Are they all obsolete because your parents moved into town?"

"We're only talking about Christmas Eve here. I thought you'd like not having to cook. You can just take it easy and enjoy yourself."

"Tradition is not left on the wayside for the sake of a few hours saved from cooking," Kathy replies. "Ask your mother about *that!*"

Karl and Kathy have been married for many years, yet there are still things they don't know about one another. Kathy didn't fully understand the Christmas traditions Karl had grown up with, nor how important those traditions are to him. Furthermore, she clearly didn't understand that he planned to incorporate those traditions into their own marriage. At the same time, Karl was unintentionally belittling the significance of the traditions he and Kathy were forming within their own nuclear family. He didn't understand the importance of

> *Traditions of our families of origin can shape who we are.*

those new traditions in his wife's mind, and the need for any changes to be discussed seriously and thoughtfully in advance.

The traditions of our families of origin have a major impact on who we are, how we think, and what we do. Openly and fully discussing family traditions, and other aspects of one's family of origin, before marriage, or at least early in marriage, reveals a great deal about oneself to one's significant other. These episodes of full disclosure go far beyond the tidbits that are gathered over the years through casual conversation. This method accelerates – and improves on – the learning process that most couples take years to complete. Not only do you learn more about your partner and their background, this process can help reveal key differences in assumptions and values so they can be discussed and resolved long before they might become a bump in the road in the years ahead.

The good news is that it's never too late to benefit from this process, so even if some of the following material may no longer be pertinent to seasoned couples, it might be interesting for you to reflect on how long it took for you and your spouse to address these subjects and how they were dealt with. You might be surprised to find some topics that still need attention.

So, where to start? It's impossible to create a truly complete list of the subject areas up for discussion. We have highlighted some of the more common – and perhaps more important – areas of interest below to give you a head start:

Finances

- What was the financial situation for your family? Wealthy? Poor? How has your perception of your family of origin's financial situation changed from when you were a child?

- How was money viewed? What was its importance and priority relative to other things in life?
- Who was responsible for paying bills and who administered the finances?
- How were decisions for major purchases made? By whom?
- Did your family have a budget? If so, how well was it followed?

Parenting

- Were both of your parents actively involved in the parenting activity? Did one parent stay home to raise the children, or was childcare used so that both parents could work?
- How was discipline of the children handled by your parents? Who did the disciplining? Was corporal punishment used? How often?
- What boundaries were set for the children? For instance, how much freedom did the children have to come and go as they pleased, and at what age? Was there a curfew? Were music, television and movie viewing monitored and restricted in terms of content and time? What effect might internet access have now?
- How much supervision of the children was required, both in the house and outside the house? How were field trips, sleepovers, and other activities that take the children away from home managed and viewed?
- How was dating managed? What age was considered old enough to date? Were there other considerations that had to be met before being allowed to date? Was there a curfew? How was transportation and money handled for dating?

- How was the topic of sex addressed with the children? At what age was *the talk* given, if at all? What was the view of pre-marital sex? How openly was this subject discussed?

Education

- How much emphasis was put on grades, and how were poor grades addressed? What was considered a poor grade?
- How was homework handled? Did your parents involve themselves by making sure it was done, or even by helping with it? Which parent handled this?
- Did you go to the local public school, or did your parents move you to another *better* public school, or even a private school?
- What were the expectations regarding college? Was it viewed as an option, or a must do?
- How were extracurricular activities viewed? Were you encouraged, or even pushed, to participate? Were you discouraged from participating?
- What did you like about the way your family handled education?
- If you could, what would you have changed about the way your family handled education?

Spirituality

- What importance did religion or spirituality have in your family of origin?
- In which faith were you raised, if any? Did you attend the same place of worship throughout your childhood? If you were not raised in a particular faith, what was your family's

view of *spirituality*?

- Was your family active in attending religious service? How often?

- Were your parents of the same faith? If not, how was this handled?

- Was your family active in the religious community? Did they volunteer for activities or ministries?

- Who was considered the *spiritual leader* of your family? Why?

- Did your family pray together, such as at dinner time?

- What did you like about the way your family viewed or practiced religion?

- If you could, what would you have changed about the way your family viewed or practiced religion?

Holidays

- Which holidays were celebrated, and were they considered a *big deal*, or just something you do on that particular date?

- Were religious holidays celebrated as religious holidays, or as an opportunity to get together with family and possibly exchange gifts?

- Where was each holiday usually celebrated? How were they celebrated?

- How did your family usually spend vacation time?

- What did you like about the way your family celebrated holidays?

- If you could, what would you have changed about the way your family celebrated holidays?

Relationships

- What was the view on living together prior to marriage?
- Was there divorce in your family? How was divorce viewed within your family?
- How were things like interracial or interfaith relationships viewed?
- Were there any incidents of extramarital affairs within your extended family? How was it viewed, and what was the outcome?

Other major life influences

- Were you raised in another country or another culture? How might cultural differences impact your choice of spouse, what you expect of your spouse, how you parent, and how you allocate your time between your new family and your family of origin?
- Were you raised by a single parent? How might this single sex influence affect your view of men? Of women?
- Did you lose a parent to death at a young age? How might this affect your choice of a mate?
- Did you have an especially dominating or especially permissive parent? Are you likely to imitate this behavior with your own children, or do the opposite?

Our families of origin form who we are and most of what we believe. Therefore, it is not surprising that – for most of us – our current views are largely shaped by the views of our parents. Of course, there are those things that we would have changed about our families of origin if we had been given the chance, and those are the areas where our own adult beliefs may differ from those of our parents, sometimes in radical ways.

Once your families of origin have been discussed openly and in detail, it's time to talk about your current thoughts and feelings in some of these same areas. If you're already married, answer each of the following questions as you would have shortly before marriage, then again based on where you are now in life's journey. Do your thoughts and feelings about the following subjects match those of your spouse or fiancée? This goes beyond simply stating what you want and what your expectations are; it is discussion and agreement on important matters. An agreement is only an agreement when both parties agree. This agreement is a core part of your marital "business plan." Take notes!

Finances

- Who will be responsible for making sure bills are paid on time?
- Who will be responsible for administering savings and investment?
- How will decisions for major purchases be made? By whom?
- What amount of money do you feel you should be able to spend without consulting with your spouse?
- Will your family have a budget? If so, what methods will be used to make sure it is followed? What actions will be taken when over-budget?

Parenting

- Will you have children? How many? When?
- If you are unable to have children of your own, will you

consider other means of becoming parents?

- Will one parent stay home to raise the children, or will childcare be used? If childcare will be used, what kind? Family? Daycare? In-home nanny?

- How will the children be disciplined? What happens if you and your spouse don't agree on the type or severity of discipline? Will one person be the final authority?

- At what age can children be left home alone?

- At what age should children be allowed out of the house unsupervised?

- At what age should children be allowed to date?

- How will the subject of sex be handled in the household? Will it be addressed as a healthy, natural part of a marriage, or a secretive, taboo subject left to the school system to address?

- What direction will you give your children relative to premarital sex?

- What message will be conveyed to the children regarding living together prior to marriage?

Education

- How will you approach education for your children? Public school? Private school? Home schooling?

- What will the expectation for higher education be? How will it be financed?

- How will report cards be handled? Will there be rewards or punishments based on the grades?

- Who will help with homework?

- Will extracurricular activities be supported? Which ones? What is the expected outcome from participation? What is their importance relative to grades and other conflicting priorities?

Spirituality

- Do you share the same beliefs? If not, how is that difference going to be handled for you as a couple, and as parents? Regardless of the strength of your faith now, children can make one's faith a more vital part of one's life. Factor this into your discussion as a *what if* scenario.
- Do you attend service together? Is it important to you for your partner to actively share your same faith and level of commitment to that faith?
- In what faith will your children be raised?
- Will you attend service on a regular basis? How often?
- Will you pray together as a family, such as at the dinner table?
- Are you actively involved in the religious community? Do you expect the same of your spouse?

Holidays

- What holidays will be celebrated, and how extravagantly?
- Where will holidays be celebrated? Whose home?
- Will religious holidays be celebrated as religious events?
- What will family vacations look like?

Some of these subject areas will come up naturally in the course of dating and normal conversation, but many will most likely be missed. In fact, some of the most important subject areas covered here probably never come up in typical dating scenarios, nor even for an engaged couple. We have known couples that stumbled into these problems after many years of marriage. For example, one couple had thoroughly discussed *when to have* children, that time being after they had accomplished specific financial goals, but they had never talked about *how to raise* children. Once they began considering getting pregnant, the wife expressed her desire to stay home with the children until they were school-age. The husband, being a product of daycare himself, as well as having an opinionated and overbearing mother, could not see the value of his wife staying home with the children and saw greater value in dual incomes. The relationship began to deteriorate as each held their ground, and sadly ended in divorce.

Taking the time to discuss these important issues, and working out differences in advance before they turn into conflicts, helps fiancées and newlyweds smoothly transition into the various stages of marital life, especially if they are reviewed periodically. For those of us that have been married for years, sharing and discussing relevant events from our families of origin continues to provide understanding about why we have the views that we do today, allowing us to learn new things about our spouses, and even about ourselves.

Respect and Leverage Your Differences

"There's one," Jill says, pointing ahead.

"I think we can do better," Jack says distractedly as his head cranes forward as if this grants him the power to see around corners. He continues to guide the minivan down the aisle of the enormous, crowded parking lot, passing the empty spot that Jill had pointed out. He gets to the end of the aisle without any luck, and circles back around just in time to see the parking space Jill had spotted being taken by a competing minivan. She grins at him, and he pretends not to notice.

"I guess I'll just have to take one of the spaces in the north forty," Jack says with a grimace. He always tries to find those up-close parking spaces, but this time it's more important than usual as a steady wind-blown rain comes down from the swollen clouds above. He parks, and they huddle under a single umbrella as they start to make their way across the expansive parking lot to the front door of the retail behemoth.

"You know," Jack says, "They really should have those trolleys like at the Disneyland parking lot to shuttle people from sections of the parking lot to the front door."

"You're right!" Jill says. "It's got to be a quarter mile away!"

"Now leaving the Rococo section...next stop Victorian," Jack says, hand curled in front of his mouth, talking into an invisible microphone.

Jack and Jill are at The Furniture Barn shopping for a new couch. They've been saving up for this splurge for a while now, and with their two boys, Jimmy and Joey, still a few years away from the highway robbery that is orthodontia, they feel okay about the expense. They're also counting it as an early present to each other, with their thirteenth anniversary just a couple months in the future.

They've been to five stores in as many hours, the rain soaking their shoes and pant legs with each stop, but Jill feels good about this one. They walk inside the labyrinthine store, grateful that their boys are off at friends' houses so they can take their time looking around without distraction.

"Can you believe this place?" Jill says, looking around the vast, cavernous space. "A person could get lost in here and never heard from again."

The store is packed with shoppers on this rainy Saturday afternoon, and Jack and Jill have to navigate a maze of people and furniture to make their way to the couch section near the back. All around them Furniture Barn salespeople are zipping around the store on Segway transporters, moving like honeybees from one customer to another.

"They should have those for the customers," Jack says as another salesperson zooms by. "I could use it to find you when you get lost."

They're thirty minutes into their exploration of the two acres of couches when Jill sees what she's been looking for.

"This is perfect," she proclaims with a look bordering on awe. "It's the perfect size, and it matches our curtains while simultaneously contrasting perfectly with our carpet."

"Didn't you say pretty much the same thing three stores ago?"

"No, I'm serious. This is it. This is what we've been looking for."

"The cushions are definitely comfy," Jack says as he settles into the plush surface, "and I think it will fit just right in the space. But don't you think the legs look a bit flimsy? You know, we haven't been to that new Smitty's Furniture Warehouse, yet. It's huge and is supposed to have a really big selection. Shouldn't we see what they have before we make a final decision?"

"No, *this* place is huge. Smitty's is in a whole different category. That place has its own zip code! Besides, I really like this sofa, and it's within our budget" Jill says. "Not to mention, if we don't get going, we'll be late meeting Karl and Kathy for happy hour. In fact, do you mind coming back tomorrow to take care of placing the order so we can get out of here?"

"Sure. No problem. I suppose it's the best one we've seen so far, anyway." Jack looks over the couch one more time before they walk away.

The next day, before heading to The Furniture Barn, Jack decides to take a quick look at Smitty's Furniture Warehouse, just in case, and discovers the perfect couch. It has the same basic colors as the one he and Jill had chosen together the previous day, it has sturdier legs, comfy cushions, and features the "Ultimate in Stain Resistance," so it must be better. *Ultimate!* Certainly, this smart choice will earn him some brownie points with Jill. As he flags down a salesperson, he decides that he won't even tell her about it so it will be a surprise when it arrives.

Jack was right. When the couch arrives, Jill is indeed surprised. "Dogs and ducks? Dogs and ducks!? Jack, I don't care that the colors are the same. How can you possibly think that a dogs-and-ducks motif works with our décor? We had agreed on the floral print from The Furniture Barn."

Jack looks at the couch with a furrowed brow. "Are those dogs and ducks? I didn't notice that. I just thought it was some kind of pattern," Jack says. "But now that you point it out, I guess they are dogs and ducks. Hunting dogs. And I think those little stripes in between them might be rifles. I guess it is a little tacky when you give it a close look."

"No kidding," Jill snaps back sarcastically. "If we were living in a hunting lodge, it'd be perfect, but not in our house. Not our beautiful house! It's got to go back. I'll go to The Furniture Barn tomorrow to order the one we saw."

"Nope," Jack says. "This was my mistake and I'll take care of it. I remember the one we chose. I just thought this one was of better quality. I'll go back tomorrow and order the floral print couch that we saw."

The next day Jack returns to The Furniture Barn and makes a beeline for the sofa he and Jill had picked out. "Did you know that this sofa is also available with a sleeper sofa option?" the salesperson asks Jack as they are writing up the order.

"Does it have sturdier legs?" Jack asks.

"No, the legs are the same."

"Then we'll stick with the regular one."

When the couch is delivered a week later, Jack and Jill stand in the living room admiring their new purchase. "Okay, I'll admit it. You were right," Jack says. "This couch does look nice in our house. Certainly, much better than the dogs-and-ducks."

Three days later, while their children, Joey and Jimmy, are roughhousing on the new sofa, one of the sofa's legs snaps in half sending the boys sprawling to the floor. No injuries, but still a scary moment.

"So, what time does Smitty's Furniture Warehouse close?" Jill asks as she wipes Jimmy's tears away. "The dogs-and-ducks are growing on me."

Jack and Jill each have their own tastes. They also each have their own set of skills and abilities. Working as a team, these sets of skills and abilities are combined to complement one another. What Jack lacks in designer flair, he makes up for in practicality. Jill may prioritize looks over durability, but her home will show more nicely for the effort. Both of those concerns are valid and important, and had Jack and Jill continued to search for the right piece of furniture, they likely would have found a piece that would meet both of their requirements. Instead, Jill won the battle of wills this time, and there was a price to pay.

When larger decisions need to be made, whether something like selecting a piece of furniture or a decision as important as a home purchase, combined effort put forth upfront will make for a better experience for the couple, and the end will be optimized. A husband and wife should take the time to sit and explore what each of them is looking for and why those things are important. Life experiences, acquired skills, and differences between the sexes give each person a unique perspective; have respect for that other perspective. Once a combined list of features, requirements, and facts is put together, the search and decision-making will go more smoothly, and possibly more quickly, as the couple works from the same list.

> *Team effort yields better outcomes.*

Tools Can Help Take the Clash Out of Decisions

Businesses use tools to make decisions every single day. In a lot of cases, using tools to assist with big decisions not only helps to lead the user to the best option, but in the Business of Marriage, it can also prevent conflict from brewing in the household. Tools are generally designed to take emotion out of the equation, and force contemplation and logic to rule.

Borrowing a technique from Operations Management, a Decision Matrix is one such tool that can assist in this process when needed. Though not practical for small, everyday matters, it can be very effective when life's larger decisions are in front of you. The Decision Matrix method ensures that the most important factors involved with a decision are given more weight, and forces the participants to evaluate all the criteria involved in that decision from an even vantage point.

Jack and Jill's friends, Darius and Delilah, have a daughter getting ready to start high school, and they want to give Deja the best education and high school experience possible. They've narrowed their choice of schools down to three possibilities, one public school and two private schools. They've looked at the financials and, though the private option will strain their budget a bit, they know they can afford it without setting themselves too far back if it makes sense, but they are unable to agree on which school is the best overall option for their daughter. They will use a Decision Matrix to help them determine an objective choice.

The key steps in using the Decision Matrix method are:

Step 1 – **Criteria List:** Create a list of all relevant criteria that either directly result from the decision or are a consequence of the decision (cost, distance, etc.). The couple should work together to build this list and include all reasonable criteria that *both* people feel are relevant. The criteria should be as objective as possible since subjective criteria will be difficult to score later in the process, though some subjective criteria may be unavoidable. Identify those criteria that are subjective to ensure they are treated as such.

<u>Step 2</u> – Weighting: Each person assigns a percentage weight to each criterion that represents the importance of that criterion to them; the total weight of all criteria must equal 100%. To make it fair, each person gets half the weighting to assign (50% per person). The process is made even more objective if the weighting assignments are written down and unseen by the other person until after the scoring step has been completed.

Criteria	Dar's wt.	Del's wt.	Ttl wt.	Public Score	Public Ttl	Private #1 Score	Private #1 Ttl	Private #2 Score	Private #2 Ttl
Distance	4%	3%	7%	4	0.28	3	0.21	2	0.14
Academic rating	3%	4%	7%	3	0.21	5	0.35	4	0.28
Teach/stud. ratio	3%	8%	11%	2	0.22	5	0.55	4	0.44
Extracurriculars	10%	5%	15%	4	0.6	3	0.45	3	0.45
Low Total Cost	12%	4%	16%	5	0.8	2	0.32	1	0.16
Friendships (subj.)	3%	5%	8%	5	0.4	4	0.32	3	0.24
Avg. SAT scores	8%	11%	19%	2	0.38	5	0.95	5	0.95
AP courses	5%	6%	11%	4	0.44	3	0.33	4	0.44
Amenities (subj.)	2%	4%	6%	4	0.24	2	0.12	4	0.24
Choice Total	50%	50%	100%		3.57		3.6		3.34

<u>Step 3</u> – Scoring: Evaluate each criterion/choice combination, and, based on how that choice matches that criterion, assign a score value from 1 to 5 based on the following:

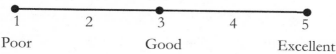

1	2	3	4	5
Poor		Good		Excellent

Only one score is assigned to each criterion/choice combination, so this must be a joint decision by the couple. Some negotiation and discussion will take place, but this is meant to be a fact-based, objective process, so only facts should be considered when applying scores.

Step 4 – Do the math: Multiply across (total weight times score) to determine total score for each criterion/choice combination, and then total the score for each choice.

Step 5 – Identify the winning choice: The best choice is the one with the highest total score. In the event of a tie between choices, consider adding additional criteria to the process and/or adjust weighting, or removing criteria that are less important, adjusting weighting to total to 100%, and rerunning the totals.

For Darius and Delilah, since all three schools made it into the comparison because they were perceived as acceptable, they are all close in terms of total score. As far as preferences, Darius put more of his weighting into Low Total Cost and Extracurriculars. Meanwhile, Delilah's scoring was distributed in a slightly more even fashion, with an emphasis in the areas of education quality (Teacher/student ratio and SAT scores). Even with Darius's heavy weighting on Low Total Cost, and the relatively high score of 5 for the Public School option, Private School #1 still received the top score of 3.6. This means that from a fairly objective perspective, all things considered, it is the best option for them. However, the close score between the top two choices may warrant a run-off matrix, to help solidify the choice, and they can feel good about removing Private School #2 from their consideration list.

Making decisions can often be a painful and stressful process. Reducing the emotion associated with a decision by using an objective technique such as the Decision Matrix will help relieve the cognitive dissonance, reduce the likelihood of finger-pointing, and defuse possible conflicts that may be arise. This results in a more informed decision and a happier marriage.

Roles and Responsibilities

Martin walks through the door after a long day at work, and his wife, Maria, can tell right away that he isn't in a good mood. He isn't the kind to complain, but she can see it in his eyes.

"Bad day, huh?" she asks.

"Not the best, but I guess it could have been worse," he replies.

"Did something happen at work?"

"The usual stuff. The day just got off on the wrong foot," he says.

"What happened?"

"You know, I really don't want to talk about it."

"You'll feel better if you do," Maria presses.

Martin hesitates before replying. "Okay. I was late for work again, for one thing." He looks at her knowingly, but she doesn't seem to notice.

"Do you need to leave a little earlier from now on?" Maria asks.

"Oh, I left with enough time to get to work on time. It just makes a big difference if I actually went straight to work when I leave the house without having to make any other unplanned stops."

"O-o-h," Maria says with a grimace.

"Considering you don't have to be at work at any specific time, doesn't it make sense for you to take Marcela to school every day?" Martin asks.

"I was going to take her, but before I knew it, you were hustling her out the door," she says defensively. "I thought you wanted to take her for some reason."

"I took her because you were still in your pajamas, and if I didn't take her when I did, she probably would have been late for school," he replies. "You know how much it stresses Marcela to have to go to the school office for a tardy slip."

"I'm really sorry," Maria says. "I definitely don't want to put more stress on Marcela. She's stressed enough thinking about starting high school next year. And I don't want you to be late getting to work."

"Well, I thank you and my boss thanks you," Martin says, smiling.

"You know I've never been a morning person, but you're right. It makes sense that I am the one who takes her to school every day, and let's agree that it's my sole responsibility. From now on, even if I have to do it in my pajamas, I will be the one to take her unless we have arranged something in advance. Deal? Kick me out the door if you have to, pajamas and all," she says with a playful smirk.

Martin looks back at her smiling.

"What?" Maria asks.

"I'm just picturing you taking Marcela to school in your pajamas. You know, the ones you bought for our anniversary trip." He raises one eyebrow and looks at her intently.

"Oh, stop it, you perv!" she says laughing, and hugs him.

Roles and responsibilities are vital for any operation to run smoothly, efficiently, and without hiccups. But what is the difference between a role and a responsibility? Roles are one-to-many relationships. That is, one person can have many different roles that they perform in their daily lives. Roles can include spouse, parent, child, employee, employer, and the list goes on.

Each role has a set of explicit and implicit responsibilities that go along with it. An explicit responsibility is one that most people will recognize, though, sadly, not everyone follows, such as parents providing food, clothing, shelter, security, and love for their children (Note: A couple that does not recognize these responsibilities is best served by putting down this book and finding professional counseling immediately). As for implicit responsibilities, they are the ones that are not hard and fast, may not have a clearly defined owner, and can often lead to problem areas for many married couples because of this ambiguity.

> *Roles & responsibilities make any operation more effective.*

Is there a way to assuage the ambiguity that comes with implicit responsibilities? It may sound pat and cliché, but clear and direct communication is the answer. A husband and wife must proactively and routinely agree on responsibility ownership, taking into account as many areas of responsibility as possible. But how does the couple divide the workload, and determine who does what?

Identifying roles and responsibilities, and aligning them to the best owner, is a way to ensure that the couple is maximizing output, minimizing inefficiency, and making the best of available resources. The resources all couples have, whether they realize it or not, include the following:

Learned Skills: Talents learned through education, training, experience, and from one's family of origin.

Natural abilities: This encompasses personality traits, as well as natural aptitudes and talents. Some people are simply better at some things than other people may be.

Bandwidth: How is time distributed relative to responsibilities? Who has available time (bandwidth) to take on an unassigned responsibility? And though *me time* is important, golf, Bunco night, and happy hours with friends shouldn't be factored into bandwidth relative to responsibilities. *Me time* is something that can be enjoyed once all responsibilities are balanced out and fulfilled.

Preferences: Though preference isn't necessarily a resource, aligning preferences to responsibilities – to the extent possible – creates efficiency, harmony, and greater job satisfaction.

There are other external resources that can be leveraged for those couples fortunate enough to have them, including assistance from extended family, hired help to the extent financially feasible, and the benefits of engaging in neighborhood and/or faith community relationships.

It is nearly impossible to divvy up implicit responsibilities if explicit responsibilities are loosely allocated, or not allocated at all. In fact, clearly defining ownership of explicit responsibilities provides the foundation for implicit responsibility assignment. In modern society, food, clothing, and shelter result from one thing: money. Unless you are living in a cave and hunting for your family's meals, at least one of you must have a job or you must be independently wealthy if you want to survive. So, the first explicit responsibility for most households is working for a living. This can be the man, the woman, or both. Once the wage-earner role is established, that information can be factored into the distribution of implicit responsibilities.

It's easy for any logical person to recognize that in a single income household, the person who is not working outside the home will carry more responsibilities inside the home. Obviously, caring for the children, being their primary source of education during those first few years, and being the CHO (Chief Household Officer), falls mostly on that stay-at-home parent. This doesn't mean that the other parent has no responsibilities in those areas, but rather that a primary owner is clearly identified. This is simply a matter of bandwidth, with the one staying at home having more available time to own those responsibilities. However, when it comes to other specific areas of implicit responsibilities, we go back to our list of resources to determine responsibility ownership. For example, who will own the task of paying the bills? Bandwidth is needed, of course, but perhaps even more important in this case are an eye for details, strong organizational skills, and an aptitude for numbers. Aligning the best resource to each responsibility is the goal.

Things are a little different when it comes to dual income homes. That primary responsibility of raising children has been partially outsourced, at least during working hours, and a full-time CHO is no longer in the picture. You now either have Joint Chiefs with equal ownership of the role, or you have no one owning the role. This puts extra strain on the distribution of responsibilities and increases the probability that each person will expect the other to pick up more slack on the home front. In this case, it is even more important to honestly examine resources to find the best owner for each responsibility, and to work together toward a solution for the family as a whole.

Let's take a look at Bob and Betty. They are a dual-income family with two grade-school-aged twin girls, Brenda and Brooke. Like most families, they have a hectic schedule, balancing work, social life, and family activities. Bob and Betty both recognize the importance of being actively involved in their children's lives and have made adjustments to accommodate that hectic schedule.

Betty feeds breakfast to the girls and gets them to school. Meanwhile, Bob has already been at work for more than an hour, having taken a work shift that allows him to be off work when the girls get out of school. Bob picks them up, feeds them a snack, and then takes them to soccer practice where he is the assistant coach.

While soccer practice is going on, Betty finishes her workday, and goes home to cook dinner. Bob and the girls get home in time to sit and have a family dinner together where they can decompress for a while and discuss their day, then it's off to do homework for Brenda and Brooke, while Bob and Betty get some alone time doing the dishes together.

With Bob's early schedule, he needs to get to sleep earlier than Betty, but they're always sure to go to bed at the same time. Betty reads for a while after Bob has fallen asleep, and in the morning, Bob always gently wakes Betty to give her a goodbye kiss before heading out, then she rolls over and gets another hour of sleep before her day gets under way.

Use Differences to Your Advantage

We cover the differences between men and women throughout this book, but the "Business of Marriage" is perhaps one area where those differences can best be leveraged. No two couples are the same, so the strengths and limitations in terms of contribution to the "business" for each individual will vary widely from couple to couple.

Truly knowing your business partner, and making a fair, honest, and thorough inventory of skills, abilities, and bandwidth, and then allocating roles and responsibilities accordingly, can ensure those differences are delivering the highest return on assets.

Once you have a good "business plan" in place, give it a chance to work for you. It may take time to begin bearing fruit, so avoid making sweeping changes too soon or too often. This doesn't mean tweaks will not be necessary, but if the plan has been well crafted it will generate results. Trust the process.

Chains do not hold a marriage together.
It is thread, hundreds of tiny threads
which sew people together through the
years.
- Simone Signoret

3

The I Dos and Don'ts

During the dating process, assuming both parties are interested in something more than a one-night stand, both the man and the woman are on their best behavior. They make an extra effort to be attractive, punctual, to use their best manners, and treat the other person with the utmost respect and courtesy. They are each out to impress the other, and this behavior is not an attempt at deception. After all, in order to fake good manners, one must know what they look like when on display and recognize their value. This is simply an instinctual attempt to make a good first impression. Being on their best behavior proves that each of them is equipped with these abilities, and believes the other person is worthy of the effort.

When these attitudes change shortly after marriage, as they too often do, it is by choice. Not necessarily a conscious choice, but the newlyweds simply feel the effort is no longer needed, or they each think the other person no longer deserves or expects that level of courtesy. But who could possibly deserve that level of respect and courtesy more than our true love? It's never too late to reintroduce the behaviors that led the married couple to the altar.

The following sections discuss some of the primary, everyday actions that collectively can help maintain some of that original spark that was there before marriage, or rejuvenate a relationship that has perhaps started to sputter a bit. Taken individually, they might seem insignificant, maybe even superficial, but together they are important ingredients to a lasting union.

Keep Yourself Attractive to Your Mate

While in the early phases of dating, each person generally invests time to look attractive to the other person. Of course, the term *attractive* means different things to different people, but we each have a notion of what we find attractive in another person, as well as things we can do to make ourselves attractive to other people. There is something about the two people in a couple that attracted them to each other in the first place, so the first step is understanding what your mate finds attractive about you and maintaining that aspect of yourself to the extent possible. The second step – and arguably the more important step – is fully recognizing that there is more to being attractive that just how one looks.

> *Being attractive goes beyond how one looks.*

Unfortunately, too many newly married people view the dating process as if it were a mountain to summit. They reach the top on their wedding day, and then get to coast down the other side without putting in as much effort. This is the wrong analogy. Dating is actually more like training for the Tour de France. Once a couple has completed the grueling training, the tournament begins on their wedding day. The real effort goes into the race, which requires the couple to maintain peak condition and performance to stay in it.

Maintaining your attractiveness for the sake of your spouse is an act of love. This extra effort on your behalf demonstrates to your spouse, and the outside world, that you respect and care about your relationship. Keeping yourself attractive makes it easier for your mate to always see you as the beautiful person they married. There is no *coasting* in marriage. The pursuit of your beloved never ends.

So, what does it mean to keep yourself attractive? After twelve years of marriage no one looks the same as they did the day vows were exchanged. Two kids and fifteen pounds later, Jill can't fit in her size-eight wedding gown anymore. Jack's wedding day tuxedo vest would now make him look like an overstuffed sausage. However, when they look at each other, they still see the person they married, and there is just as much mutual attraction as there was when they were dating. Why is this?

For one thing, Jill spends the time to put on a little makeup every day; even on days she isn't going to see anyone else in the world but Jack and the kids. Gaining fifteen pounds is not all that scary, and isn't surprising for a mother of two, but Jill continues to eat a healthy diet and exercises regularly. She has set a rule that she will not allow herself to buy the next size up in clothes, which keeps her in check. These things make Jack love her even more, not for how she looks, but for this expression of love she is putting forth for him.

For Jack, he still puts on just a touch of cologne when going on a date with his wife, knowing she is the only one who will get close enough to smell it. He still goes to the gym three times a week in an attempt to maintain some semblance of youthful vigor. Additionally, though the daily shaving ritual was left behind, he won't let too many days string together without dragging a razor across his face, or at least going at it with a beard trimmer. Jill notices, and finds it endearing, constantly drawing her closer to him.

But attractiveness — and being *sexy* — goes well beyond how you look, what you wear, your weight, or any other physical attribute. Sexy also has a lot to do with your behavior and the message it conveys to the opposite sex. Imagine if on the day you reach dating age you are handed a large bag filled with sand, and that "sexy sand," each and every grain, represents your sex appeal. While the bag is full, you are at your maximum level of sexy. The bag is a little heavy, the sexy sand is a bit of a burden to lug around, but you do it gladly, being careful not to lose one single grain of the precious sand. When in the presence of this new person who has come into your life, this person that might or might not someday share a bed and a name with you, you're careful about the way you look, but you're also careful to say the right things, do the right things, and not do the wrong things. Then your wedding day comes and goes, and before you know it, you're behaving in ways that punch holes in the bag, letting the sexy sand run out, and your sex appeal with it.

While dating, most women would run for the hills if the man thought it humorous to "let one rip" in her presence. Most men know this, so they are on their best biological behavior during that critical stage. Apparently, something happens to the sphincter muscle in many males shortly after marriage. The control is just not there, anymore. The man fools himself into thinking that the marriage certificate somehow removed the vulgarity of this biological event, or somehow rendered his wife both deaf and without a sense of smell; however, the woman is still just as horrified as she would have been during the dating stage. And guess what guys, that behavior doesn't fall into the category of sexy, no matter how ripped your abs might be, and you just punched a huge hole in your bag of sex appeal. The sexy sand is pooling around your feet, and there's no putting it back.

As for women, many of you have a monthly biological event that, as natural and beautiful as it is to you, most men simply don't want to think about, talk about, or know about. Being present to witness the "changing of the guard" during those few days each month is not at the top of the list for most men as far as sexy visual images. Every time you let your man witness this activity you are punching holes in your bag of sex appeal, and all the king's horses and all the king's men can't put the bag back together again.

Before Jack had married Jill – in fact, before Jack had even met Jill – a friend of Jack's shared a story with him shortly after the friend had gotten married. The friend had been married about a month when, one morning while he was standing at the bathroom mirror shaving, his new wife walked into their small bathroom, pulled down her pajama bottoms, sat on the toilet and took care of business. As this friend tells it, "That's when I knew the honeymoon was over."

No matter how you try to dress it up, certain bodily functions are best left as your alone time. It isn't romantic, and it isn't a symbol of intimacy to share the moment. Even in medieval times, people had the courtesy to go behind a tree, and we like to think we've made some progress in this new-fangled era of indoor plumbing and hinged doors. It's probably safe to assume that the sexy sand belonging to that friend's wife ran dry early in marriage, regardless of the fact that she was an attractive looking woman.

Bedtime attire opens a whole new area for defining what is attractive and what isn't. Modest, yet loose, tank-top pajamas on the woman: attractive. A facial peel mask and long-sleeved flannel on the same woman: not as attractive. Fifties style white briefs, knee high socks, and a white tank-top undershirt on the man: definitely not attractive. Fashionable boxers and nothing else on the same man: attractive.

Attraction means different things to different people. What's important is knowing what makes you attractive to your specific mate, and what they might find unattractive, even if you have to ask them to find out. Then, maintain those aspects of your person for the good of your marriage, and for the love of your spouse.

Minimizing the Criticizing

Jill is out to lunch with her friends Betty and Delilah. As usual they are sharing stories about their children and their husbands.

"So, did everyone have a nice Mother's Day last week?" Jill asks.

"I had a nice, relaxing day. Bob and the girls made breakfast in bed for me, and then we went for a hike in the afternoon," Betty says.

"That sounds wonderful," Jill says. "How about you, Delilah?"

"It was okay, I guess. Darius made Mother's Day breakfast as usual, and then you won't believe what he did!"

"What?" Jill and Betty reply together.

"He gave me a bracelet. And I know he bought it on Saturday, because he mysteriously went to 'run some errands' that morning. He never runs errands Saturday morning. I mean, the day before Mother's Day!" Delilah says. "I know he had a busy week at work last week, but it wasn't like Mother's Day was a surprise. It's the same Sunday every year!"

Jill and Betty quietly listen.

"Then he gives me a bracelet that I didn't ask for, and spent way too much money on it," Delilah says. "I had just told him three weeks ago how I could use a day at the spa. Can't he take a hint?"

"I know what you mean," Betty says. "Bob seems to be in his own world sometimes, so any hints fall on deaf ears."

"If he paid more attention to me, he'd know that I never even wear bracelets," Delilah says

"But, when it comes to a gift, isn't it the thought that counts?" Jill asks.

"Obviously, he *wasn't* thinking!" Delilah says. "Otherwise, I would be telling you all about my appointment at the spa this coming weekend."

How many times do we go to lunch with our friends and it turns into a spouse-bashing session? What they do wrong, what they don't do right, and what they should do the way *we* do it! In some circumstances, venting may be the right thing to do, as it lets off steam, getting some of the frustration out of the system. However, venting about your spouse with a sympathetic group, such as your friends or family, may just add fuel to a smoldering fire. Of course, they are going to agree with you; they're your friends and family! But is it fair to your spouse since they are not present to defend themselves, or offer their version of the story? Is it productive to bash, or does it just inflate the issues from your perspective, raising your ire and your blood pressure? Do you ever think about the behaviors and habits that you display that may be objectionable or annoying to your spouse? For that matter, do you spend time really considering their side of things?

In the case of Delilah's husband, Darius, the "busy week" she is referring to was much worse than she realizes. In fact, it was a busy two weeks in which Darius almost lost his job, and had to really scramble to convince his boss to keep him on. He didn't tell Delilah about it because he didn't want to spoil her Mother's Day. He had every intention of shopping earlier in the week, but with this situation at work, he simply wasn't able to. When he did go shopping, he searched for hours for just the right gift. He eventually saw the bracelet and thought it was beautiful and would look amazing on his wife's wrist. He thought the fact that she didn't own any bracelets would make it even more special.

Sometimes spouse-bashing takes place even with the spouse present and just a few feet away. A while back we were attending a dinner party with a few other couples, when out of the blue one of the wives asked the other husbands present about whether or not they cursed at other drivers on the road. She went on to explain how her husband got extremely riled up over the actions of other drivers, and that she was worried that he would become either a victim, or perpetrator, of road rage. She said that she was worried about him, and worried about the kids when they're in the car with him, and that when she asks him to stop behaving this way, he doesn't stop.

Faced with this public trial, of course the husband denied the charges, saying that his wife was exaggerating the facts. The wife then proceeded to poll the rest of the men present on whether they behaved the same way when driving, and whether or not they'd stop if their wives asked them to.

Obviously, the wife's concern for her husband is valid since road rage is very real, and you just never know who is driving that other car. Yet, this was the wrong forum for this discussion, especially with him being caught totally by surprise. Anyone in his place would feel that they were under attack, exposed, and become very defensive. Furthermore, her action only succeeded in turning a pleasant dinner party into an intervention session, angering her husband, and making the rest of the group somewhat uncomfortable. Had she handled this issue in a more private, relaxed environment, taking the time to really explain her feelings and fears to the husband, she likely would have gotten a better result.

Another area of concern relative to criticism resides squarely at home. Never criticize your spouse in front of, or to, your children, regardless of their age. Just don't do it. Your children need to see their parents as a united front. When a child sees a lack of unity, it creates feelings of insecurity and anxiety, it can lower the respect the child has for the parents, and ultimately manifest itself in behavioral issues. Little ears should be out of range before any confrontation between the parents can take place, regardless of intensity.

When it comes to your spouse, the *only* person you should do this kind of venting with *is* your spouse. We're not talking about unproductive criticizing or bickering, but rather a grounded, respectful discussion of the issues at hand. Approach matters as they come up; don't let them build. Here are a few suggestions that have resulted in successful conflict resolution in our own marriage:

- Choose neutral ground such as a restaurant or park. It's not uncommon for certain parts of a home to tend to be *more hers* or *more his* in a person's mind, and you want to completely remove even the perception of a home field advantage. This also ensures that the children are out of earshot, in case it's an intense matter.

- At the meeting, whoever called the meeting describes the issue and solicits input from the other person first, so it doesn't come across as simply an attack. This is a way to get more information on the matter at hand before continuing the conversation, and it gives the other person a chance to raise any other issues, as well, therefore creating a dialog rather than a confrontation.

- The encounter requires quiet listening, not confrontation. Always let the other person finish what they are saying before chiming in.

- Converse as if you are coworkers or professional associates. The same rules and etiquette apply.

- If it's clear that you have wronged or hurt the other person, apologize. An apology is not a sign of weakness, it is a sign of respect and love for the other person, and can quickly diffuse a tense situation.

- Give fair warning. If the topic at hand makes you have feelings of anger, start the conversation with something like, "There's something that's making me feel angry, and I want to talk to you about it." The other person then knows to take you very seriously, and it establishes the Rules of Engagement.

- Don't set traps. Avoid talking *around* the issue, waiting for your mate to step into the jaws of death. Just like in the courtroom, there should be no unfair surprise once the *trial* has started.

- Address the issues or behavior, not the person. Avoid the word *you*. Absolutely never call names or use negative, accusatory language, and never say things that are hurtful and can't be taken back.

- Remember that compromise is an important part of marriage. This doesn't mean one of you simply gives in. Too much of that and the *giver in* quickly becomes a doormat. Rather, to the extent possible, find a result that works for both of you. Think outside the box with an eye for the creative. There is often more than one way to resolve a problem than is immediately obvious. Also, the priority is finding a solution, not a winner.

- Stay away from the "F" word. That is, don't let the word *fault* enter into the conversation. Where to place blame, whether directing it at the other person or yourself, has no place in working as a team, nor in finding the best outcome.

- Before departing, use pen and paper to document the solution you have formulated so you can refer back to it. Use plenty of detail so that you capture not just the decision, but the feeling that surrounded the decision.

- Follow through to make sure you meet your commitments. Take the issue seriously, because you can bet that your mate certainly does.

Criticizing your spouse can be habit forming, and unfortunately, like many habit-forming drugs, sometimes the more you do it, the more you need to do it. The key is to have enough respect for your spouse to completely avoid the behavior from the beginning, or if you are already down the criticizing path, go cold turkey and stop immediately. Applying the golden rule makes for a good marriage: "Speak of others as you would have them speak of you."

Be Polite to Your Spouse

Manners are not just for other people. They aren't something you put on display for the outside world to show off your knowledge of etiquette, but rather a way to show respect and consideration for the people around you. Is there anyone who merits that more than your spouse?

Manners are not just for outside the home.

For any of you who may have forgotten what manners are, they are those behaviors our parents tried to teach us over the course of our childhoods, generally accompanied by disapproving looks, sometimes the *evil eye*, and expressions of general exasperation. Hopefully, for most of us, at least some of those lessons stuck, and, though some natural relaxing of the niceties is normal as a couple becomes more comfortable with one another, there is a baseline of good manners that must always remain intact. For example, while it is okay to chew with your mouth full, or talk with your mouth open, it is not okay to chew with your mouth open, or talk with your mouth full, regardless of how long you've been married.

Remember that the children are watching and listening, so teach by example. The way you treat your spouse is very likely how your children will treat their own spouses when their time comes, and how they will expect to be treated. *Please* and *Thank You* are some of the very first things we teach our children. Do you expect better manners from your children than you expect from yourself, or from your spouse? If not, remember your manners and use them at all times, especially in front of your children.

Even though it's very normal for some manners to relax some after marriage, here are just a few that we try to hold onto even with our stroll down the aisle decades behind us:

- Of course, please and thank you
- A gentleman always opens the door for a lady, no matter who that lady is
- Even when please is used, some ways of asking are more polite than others. "Would you take out the trash for me, please?" as opposed to "Take out the trash, please." The request needs to be in the form of a question, rather than just a command with a nice *please* added at the end. The "for me" acknowledges that you recognize the other person is doing something on your behalf, and the "would you" further softens the request.

- Keep bodily noises to yourself. They are never as cute or humorous as you might think they are, and we're not just talking to the men here.

- Always be considerate. Don't be the one who grabs the last potato chip, biscuit, or last kernel of popcorn. Always offer it to the other person first, even if you secretly hope they'll turn it down. If you're on the receiving end, sometimes turn it down, but it's okay to sometimes take it so the other person feels good about making the offer.

This list is not all-encompassing, of course. For most people, common sense will help you navigate situations to make sure the best side of you is on display. But just as familiarity breeds contempt, familiarity can also interfere with common sense and common manners. Recognize when this is happening and make course corrections.

Don't Go to Bed Without Your Spouse

Few things embody the essence of marriage like the act of retiring to a shared bed at the end of each day, regardless of what you do once you get there. Unfortunately, many couples find their routines gradually going in different directions, ultimately reaching the point where they kiss goodnight in the kitchen, and the next time they see each other in the waking world is in the morning, or even the following afternoon if one of them is an early riser with an early work schedule. Having different bedtimes can happen for a lot of reasons, some of them unavoidable, however, perpetuating this behavior, and letting it become a habit, gradually erodes the relationship and the roles of husband and wife. Before you know it, you're just roommates whose paths happen to cross on occasion.

After all the hustle and bustle of the day, once the children are asleep and the house has quieted, this is a great opportunity to have an *adult moment* with your spouse. We aren't just talking about sex, although with luck you can work that in, too, but rather time for adult conversation, decompression, and emotional intimacy. Okay men, don't get scared. We aren't necessarily talking about a lot of talking and getting in touch with your feminine side. We're talking about discussion of the day's events from a parents' perspective, planning for the next day's schedule, other things that have come up that require some "melding of the minds," and all the while you can be holding hands or entwining legs or touching feet. Making some form of skin contact adds a great deal to the intimacy of the moment and encourages both parties to feel like part of one whole.

Just to be clear, we are not saying that bedtime is the only time, or even the best time, for couples to discuss important family issues. In fact, bedtime is not a good time to get into serious discussion on a very serious topic since you are probably in bed to get some sleep. Bedtime is the time for *winding down* conversation, the important components being the physical closeness and the casual interaction. If that leads to even more physical closeness, good for you!

Make Your Spouse Feel Secure in Your Marriage

Humans are territorial creatures, and jealousy can happen in any relationship. A marriage built on trust can more easily rise above the disputes brought on by petty jealousy, however, this doesn't mean one can rest on one's laurels. Maintaining trust takes continued diligence, restraint, and the ability to recognize potentially dangerous, trust-reducing situations.

Temptation can sometimes be disguised as a wolf in sheep's clothing. Many acts of infidelity – whether physical or emotional infidelity – begin through casual contact with a coworker, business associate, or family friend. As long as the contact stays casual, there's no problem. When casual contact makes the leap to a compromising situation, recognizing it and taking evasive action is critical to the stability and future of your marriage.

Spending too much time alone with someone of the opposite sex makes even the most understanding spouse a bit concerned, and the more time spent with that person, the more likely that perceived impropriety, emotional infidelity, or even a romantic advance on the part of one party or the other may happen. The following situations are red flags when they involve you *being alone with someone of the opposite sex* who is not your spouse:

- going out of town overnight on business
- frequent lunch or dinner meetings
- regular late nights at work together
- sharing marital issues as a confidant
- showing a visiting old friend around town
- internet chatrooms
- repeated phone calls or texting

Doing any of these things doesn't mean you're having an affair, or even that you are going to have an affair if you don't stop. However, they can certainly lead you down a bad path and open the window of opportunity for making bad decisions. Furthermore, these situations may give the *appearance* of impropriety, and begin piercing the shield of trust your spouse has in you.

If you must put yourself in an isolated situation that could be misinterpreted by an outside observer, or that you think your spouse could misinterpret if informed by a third party, tell your spouse about the encounter in advance. If you do find yourself in this type of situation, and it is causing friction in your marriage, be prepared to make changes, possibly even a career change, if necessary. This is not about trust or over-reaction. Anyone in your spouse's shoes may feel the same way. What are you willing to do to protect your marriage?

At the same time, both spouses must be diligent about controlling misplaced *dis*trust and always allow sound reason to rule. There is a delicate balance between the trust you have in your spouse and the caution that must be exercised to prevent external forces from negatively affecting your relationship, whether those forces are acting with malice or not. A good general rule for any marriage, whether related to fidelity or any other matter of trust, is to assess the situation in relation to your spouse's character. If you are perceiving a trust-threatening situation that falls completely outside what you know to be your spouse's normal character, you must allow room for the possibility that you are misreading the situation. Give them the benefit of the doubt and approach the matter accordingly.

Many years earlier, while Jill and Jack were working at the same company and in the same building, there was a time when Jill needed to go to a business lunch with her boss, Leonard, whom Jack knew well. As Jill was leaving the building, she popped in to let Jack know that she and Leonard were heading to lunch. About an hour later, Jack got a call from a buddy of his who said, "Hey Jack, I just saw your wife out to lunch with some dude." This well-meaning buddy wasn't trying to stir up trouble, but merely watching out for his friend's interests. Had Jack not known who Jill had gone to lunch with and under what circumstances, this could have resulted in a heated discussion that evening, regardless of how innocent the situation actually was. With full disclosure in advance, the situation simply resulted in a funny anecdote for them to laugh about later that day.

Trust is something that is earned slowly over time beginning when a relationship first starts. It can be lost quickly through a single isolated act of selfishness, or it can be lost slowly through repeated questionable behavior. A series of compromising situations on the part of Spouse A, although they may be perfectly innocent, puts Spouse B in a vulnerable position which is damaging to the marriage.

> *Trust is lost quickly with selfishness, or slowly through poor choices.*

This pattern of behavior can gradually erode trust, creating an unstable environment in the home. There may be times when this type of scenario cannot be avoided for a short amount of time, such as a work or school project, and Spouse A needs to be sensitive to the feelings and perceptions of Spouse B and not just casually dismiss any concerns that are raised. Getting angry about your spouse being concerned about the situation isn't productive. If you put yourself in a position that could make your spouse feel insecure, and you don't proactively take the steps to mitigate their concerns, the blame falls squarely on you.

The appearance of impropriety can be a bit subjective. At the end of the day, it takes common sense and awareness to recognize when you have landed in a potentially dangerous situation. Here are a few tests that you can use to identify them:

- Would you be comfortable if your spouse was in the same situation or made the same decision?
- Is the situation something you'd hesitate in telling your spouse about, worried that they might get the wrong idea?
- Could the situation be misinterpreted as being inappropriate when viewed by a third party?
- If a friend of yours of the same sex were in the same situation, would you wonder if they were *up to something*?

Trust is a cornerstone of happy marriage. Using these guidelines will help shield your relationship from many of the sources of misplaced distrust and insolate you from making a potentially marriage-killing mistake. However, infidelity – both physical and emotional – has many avenues, and both you and your spouse must remain vigilant to protect the sanctity of your relationship.

Putting It All Together

Our insights and recommendations for most of the topics we have covered in this chapter may sound like common sense. Most people should be able to figure this out on their own, right? Or maybe these ideas sound old fashioned. Unfortunately, with the everyday pressures, comings and goings, and the natural "settling into a groove" that happens as a relationship matures, many people simply don't have these things on their mind, or they think of them after damage has already been done. But, respect, courtesy, and common sense never go out of fashion. It's often those old-fashioned ideas that -- when ignored -- spring up to surprise marriages and throw them into very modern bad situations.

Marriage is hard work. Good marriage is even harder, but the payoff is worth the effort. Once you have trained yourself to use these techniques, or follow these guidelines, they will eventually become habit. However, watch for backsliding. If you find yourself treating coworkers or friends better than you're treating your spouse, immediate attention is needed.

The ideal husband understands every
word his wife doesn't say.
- Alfred Hitchcock

4

Boys Will Be Boys and Girls Will Be Girls

In decades past a person went to the movie theater to escape the realities of life, take a break from their own world, and be entertained for a couple hours. This worked fine when the person could leave the fantasy world of film behind and recognize reality when they pushed their way back through the double doors. Unfortunately, modern society has taken "life imitates art" too far in many areas. Our modern media culture creates many unrealistic expectations, often setting relationships up for failure.

One hundred years ago, young people created their vision of what their wedding and married life would be like based on their own observations, what they had been told by friends and family, and perhaps from books. The firsthand accounts, though perhaps rose colored by memory, were rooted in reality. As for books, the words simply stimulated the reader's imagination based on their own perceptions. Movies, on the other hand, don't give a person that opportunity. All the details and blanks are filled in for the viewer, including beautiful people, impeccable settings, and every couple in perfect tune with one another, if the screenwriter chooses to make it that way. Or, even if there is turmoil in the script, everything gets worked out to perfection before the two hours is over. With this imagery spoon-fed to a person, there is no room left for imagination or personal interpretation. Once television came along, the situation worsened as young men and women were immersed in this unreal world on a daily basis from a very early age. The internet and social media simply added fuel to the fire.

Where does that leave us? To meet that new ideal of what a spouse and married life should look like, the man must always be in perfect physical condition, always well-groomed with perfectly mussed hair, dressed in the latest fashion, wake up in the morning freshly shaven and with minty fresh breath, and always aware of his woman's needs. And no matter what industry the man works in, or what job he holds, he always gets home while it's still light outside, with just enough time to throw the ball with his son before the gourmet dinner is served by his doting wife.

Meanwhile, the woman must be shaped like a Barbie doll, dress like a Victoria's Secret model (even after having three children), wakeup looking like she just came from the beauty salon and wearing a sexy nightie even in the middle of winter, and have the same minty fresh breath that her husband somehow maintains through hours of bacteria-breeding sleep. A woman must also have the ability to sprint after her toddler across a gravel parking lot while wearing a pencil skirt and five-inch stiletto heels. And let's not forget the matching his-and-hers

Mercedes sedans in the garage.

Now let's take a step back into reality. We simply cannot live up to the standard set by Hollywood, nor should we want to when we consider their track record for real-life relationships. Real marriage is chock full of trials and tribulations, a smattering of unachieved goals, and the cold bucket of water over the head realization that one must put another human being's needs above one's own. A husband and wife have to

> *Marriage takes work, but it leads to shared accomplishment.*

work at marriage, and while the word *work* seems to have negative connotations for some people, it is simply the act of creating, building, or improving something, or just maintaining something that is already in good shape. In marriage, this is not an individual endeavor, but rather a team effort. Teamwork brings people together, and it is teamwork that gives a couple feelings of joint accomplishment and pride in their relationship.

Like any team, each member has different strengths, weaknesses, capabilities, and personalities. In football, if all eleven players on a team are quarterbacks, that team will not be bringing home the big trophy. A football team needs a variety of players on both offense and defense to effectively compete. In the husband-wife team, each person is different, and these differences need to be understood, and even capitalized on, for the good of the team. To work together effectively, couples need to recognize, embrace, and celebrate humanity and the differences between men and women. Once we do that, we can finally truly fall in love with our spouses, rather than with that virtual ideal of what we think we want.

A Man Doesn't Think Like a Woman

Karl and Kathy look forward to Friday as much as anyone. On one such Friday afternoon, Kathy calls her husband at work to touch base on some family business, and before finishing the conversation says to him, "Let's go out tonight. I'll call the babysitter if you'll take care of the other arrangements." After hanging up with Kathy, Karl begins making some calls, but is interrupted when he is requested at a last-minute meeting.

That unexpected meeting has Karl running a little late on his drive home to suburbia, and as if that's not enough, traffic is worse than usual. He is most of the way home when he realizes that he forgot to make the restaurant reservation. He quickly makes the call from the car, and is relieved to hear that there's still a table available. Whew, close one!

When Karl finally gets home, he finds that Kathy has held up her part of the bargain. The babysitter, Stacy, has already arrived and is in the family room watching a movie with their boys, Kyle and Kirk, who are already in their pajamas.

"Hey guys!" Karl says to the trio on the couch. "Happy Friday! Did you have a good day at school?"

"Yes," the boys reply in unison.

"Do you have a lot of homework this weekend?"

"No," comes the synchronized response.

"Well, good. Do you know where your mom is?"

Kyle, the nine-year-old, replies, "She said she was going upstairs to get ready for your daaaaate," turning the word "date" into a four-syllable word. "She's been up there a loooong time," he says, making a face.

"Okay. You boys be good for Stacy, and I expect to find you

both asleep by the time we get home," Karl says.

"Awwwww!" the boys exclaim in unison, as Karl walks away with a smile on his face. He wants them asleep before he and Kathy get home to improve the odds of makeup sex; that is, sex that happens before she can remove her makeup and put on her flannel pajamas. Once she's in those pajamas, they don't come off until morning.

Karl heads upstairs to get ready for their outing, and, walking into the bedroom, he can see Kathy's reflection in the bathroom mirror across the room, putting the finishing touches on her makeup. He's a bit surprised to see that she's wearing her little black dress, has gone all out with her makeup, including mascara on her eyelashes, and her small evening purse is lying on the bed. Perhaps a good detective would have put two and two together, but that was never Karl's strength. So, brow furrowed, he asks her, "What are you all dressed up for?"

"Ha Ha! You're so funny!" Kathy says flatly, but with a smile. "Hurry up and get ready. You're late!"

"No, really. Aren't you a little overdressed?" Karl asks.

Kathy pauses, and without turning around, looks at Karl in the mirror with a puzzled expression. "What do you mean? I thought we were going out tonight for a nice dinner."

Karl enters the closet to grab his clothes for the evening, as he says, "But I called Jack, and he and Jill are going to meet us at Red Robin for a burger and some beer. I got reservations for four people."

The prolonged silence that serves as a response from his wife causes the first warning bells to begin going off in the deep recesses of Karl's brain. His head pops back out of the closet, and a worried look surfaces in his eyes as he tries to read his wife's face in the mirror's reflection.

Cautiously, he fully exits the closet and continues to watch Kathy's face as she stares at herself in the glass. She notices him behind her, and her eyes flick toward him, then she slowly turns to face him. Karl subtly shifts from foot to foot, trying to avoid the fire in those eyes, while also trying not to look away. Kathy finally responds between slightly clenched teeth, articulating each word. "I thought we were going out tonight."

"We…are?" It starts as a statement but finishes as a question.

"Red Robin with Jack and Jill is your idea of a romantic evening out? I thought we were going someplace nice, someplace with seafood, and wine that has to be opened with a corkscrew. And, I didn't even know you could make reservations at Red Robin!"

"You know, there are many fine wines these days with screw tops, including at Red–"

"Are you kidding right now?" Kathy interrupts, eyes smoldering.

"Well, how was I supposed to know that was what you wanted to do?" he exclaims.

"I shouldn't have to tell you!"

"Well, apparently you do!"

From the same sentence, "Let's go out tonight", Karl and Kathy had two completely different images of what that evening would look like. Kathy assumed that Karl knew exactly what she meant by *arrangements* when she made the proposal. However, the definition of *a good time* is very different between most men and women. If left to their own devices, men revert to cavemen and seek to satisfy their more primal urges. Maslow's hierarchy of needs tells us that — on the most fundamental level — men will seek air, water (we'll substitute beer here), food, shelter, sleep, and sex. We'll add to that the man's need for male bonding and *tool talk*.

Therefore, for men a fun evening out might constitute a large burger and beer with friends, followed by sex-induced sleep. Jeff Foxworthy says it best. To paraphrase Jeff, a man's definition of *romance* is "a beer and something naked." Adding to that, while for women *intimacy* may be hugs and quiet conversation, for a man it may mean sneaking up behind his wife and grabbing her boobs in a playful way. This isn't necessarily a sexual thing, but just gives him the feeling that he's getting away with something. There is a boy lurking inside every man.

Not only do men and women think differently when confronted with a specific issue or decision, at almost any point in time their brains may be processing what is coming through all their senses in different ways. The stimuli may hit the sensory receptors in the same way, but how the brain processes those nerve impulses is influenced by differences in gender, experiences, associations, and even one's emotional state at that moment. Consider the following conversation between Karl and Kathy, several months after the Red Robin incident, as an example:

> Men and women usually define "a good time" differently.

"You know, you look so beautiful by the light of the dashboard," Karl says.

Kathy takes a quick look over at her husband to make sure he's being serious, then gets her eyes back on the road. "Awww, that's so sweet. I hope that's not just beer goggle talk," she replies, smiling.

Karl and Kathy are on their way home after a fun party at the home of their friends, Jack and Jill. Over the years, they've developed a routine for taking turns being designated driver, and tonight was Kathy's turn, so she's smoothly navigating the SUV through the quiet residential streets on the short drive home. Neither of them is a big drinker, but better safe than sorry, and it seems that Karl might have had more than his customary two drinks on this particular Saturday evening. They've also begun their other routine of comparing notes on their observations from the party.

"So, what did you think about the food?" Karl asks.

"I thought the food was pretty good," Kathy says.

"Yeah, Jack and Jill really know how to put on a party. Always plenty to eat and drink," Karl says. "I need to get a copy of that playlist Jack had going. Great music."

"It seems like there were a few new faces at this one," Kathy says.

"Yep, I think Jack invited some people from work this time."

"Did you see the woman in the leather pants? Do you have any idea who she is?"

"You mean the one helping Jill pass out the snacks?" Karl asks.

"Snacks? You mean the hors d'oeuvres?"

"Yeah, those little bite thingies."

"No, not her. Those weren't even leather pants. I'm talking about the one hanging around the bar all evening. She was wearing tight leather pants and stiletto heels," Kathy says, "and she had on a tube-top of all things," she finishes with a laugh.

"What year does she think this is?"

Karl considers this. "Hmmm. I don't think I noticed her."

"How did you not notice her, dressed like that?"

"Sorry, hon, I guess I just missed her." Karl says with a shrug.

After a few minutes of silence, Karl asks, "Say, did you see Sam's new girlfriend? You know, the blond with the big boobs? I think she was wearing black pants. I certainly didn't miss *her!*"

"I didn't miss her either! She's the one I'm talking about! I suppose the big boobs are all you saw. You didn't notice that she was dressed like a stripper from 1980?" exclaims Kathy.

"Yeah…I was thinking exactly the same thing." Karl says, innocently. "Stripper from the eighties. Yuck."

"And, I bet those boobs aren't even real!"

"Yeah, big fake boobs. Double yuck," Karl says, giving his wife a quick sideways glance.

In an attempt to sidestep that minefield, he quickly changes the subject, "Hey, did you see Jack's new subwoofer? I was thinking about asking Santa for one this Christmas."

"Of course, I saw it. Jack was showing it off to everyone. Personally, I thought the music was too loud and thumpy. I can't believe Jill went along with putting that woofy-thingy in her beautiful living room."

"I thought the music sounded great, and it probably sounds amazing for watching movies, too," Karl says.

"It's just a big, black, ugly cube sitting in the living room."

"So, you didn't like it?"

"Why would I like it? It's looks tacky!" Kathy says.

Karl suddenly finds the good vibrations from the party quickly fizzling away, along with his dreams of a Christmas subwoofer. *How many months until Christmas? Surely, she'll forget about Jack's subwoofer by then, right?*

After a moment of silence, Karl asks, "Have I mentioned how beautiful you look by the light of the dashboard?"

Karl and Kathy saw the same things at the party, but because they are different people, and more importantly, because they are of the opposite sex, they perceived them in a totally different way. These different perspectives caused friction as Kathy was put-off by the fact that Karl didn't see things the same way, and therefore couldn't provide the affirmation she sought.

Women can save themselves and their husbands a great deal of pain and suffering if they will acknowledge that their husbands' minds work in a very different way. Women need to understand that a husband having a different perspective does not mean that he loves his wife less (the *"if you loved me, you would know"* syndrome), or that he is being insensitive. He's just being a man.

> *Your spouse doesn't know what you're thinking; tell them.*

When Kathy called Karl to arrange a night out, she obviously had something specific in mind. Her expectations would have been better met if she had told Karl exactly what she had in mind. A woman assuming a man will know what she's thinking is a recipe for disaster. Here are some traits most men possess which women are well served to keep in mind:

Men tend to have a simple, linear way of thinking. They analyze situations and look for logical, practical solutions or answers.

- When their son is confronted with a bully teasing him at school, the father says, "Make sure there are witnesses, tell the bully to throw the first punch, then let him have it." Meanwhile, the mother's plan is to meet with the principal, talk to the parents of the bully, and counsel her son on the old sticks-and-stones philosophy.

Men and women react to situations differently, especially when there is emotion involved.

- If a woman sees a coworker crying (man or woman), she gets concerned for that person, asks what's wrong and offers her comfort and support.

- A man in the same situation checks the location of all exits, breaks out in a cold sweat, and pretends not to notice.

- On the other hand, if a man sees his wife crying, he thinks *Uh oh, what did I do?* before he even knows what's going on. And regardless of the situation, he hopes it will end up in "make up sex" (not to be confused with the aforementioned *makeup sex*).

Men have a very different emotional construction.

- Men are more physical and express their emotions through action. This explains why most men are sports fanatics.

- Men often channel their emotions through the activity of love making.

- For men, sex is a way for them to show love for their wife, as well as a demonstration of their strength and ability to physically protect their woman. It's also their way of saying "Mine!"

- Men don't understand that women don't operate the same way, and no amount of telling them will make a difference.
- The way to a man's heart is not through his stomach. You need to travel a little further south.

Men almost always have less to say than women.
- Don't expect him to contribute half of the conversation.
- Just because he's not talking, it doesn't mean he is ignoring you, or that he is not interested in what you're saying. It also doesn't mean he's angry, worried, contemplative, introspective, ill, or having an affair. He's probably just watching mental reruns of last night's football game.
- If you don't provide at least 75% of the conversation, he'll think you're mad at him about something, which may cause him to be even quieter.

Men can't read women's minds and will never be able to think like a woman.
- Don't set mind-traps. If there's something you want your husband to know, do, or say...tell him! If you had a teleprompter built into your forehead, life would be so much easier for him, but without it you are left in charge of feeding him the lines like Cyrano de Bergerac.
- For example, if you are expecting a special anniversary outing including a particular restaurant, a particular gift, and all the bells and whistles, don't simply say "it would be nice to go out for a nice dinner for our anniversary," leaving it up to him set up the perfect evening. Give him specifics so that he has the opportunity to please you. "For Friday, you'll need

to make reservations at Pierre's as soon as possible. And do you remember that watch I showed you last weekend? That is a perfect anniversary gift for me. I'll take care of arranging the babysitter and make sure your blue suit is back from the cleaners so you can wear it."

Men and women may appear to be spawned from different species, but given the right loving direction, with plenty of gentle clues and cues, men can be coaxed into responding to their wives' emotional, physical, and social needs. At the same time, by recognizing that her husband's brain functions in a different way, a wife is better equipped to interpret her husband's cues and emotions, enabling her to better fulfill his expectations of the relationship.

A Woman Doesn't Think Like a Man

Karl arrives home from work, and as usual, he can't pull into the driveway without first getting out of the car and moving bicycles, various sports paraphernalia, and the other accessories that make up boyhood activities from the middle of the driveway.

Car finally tucked away in the garage, Karl walks into the house, stopping to shuffle through the day's mail laying on the side table near the door, as he does every day.

"Honey, I'm home," he calls out, comfortably using this cliché that is also part of his daily routine. He passes by the family room where the boys are watching the television in a trance-like state.

"Hey, guys! How was your day?"

"Good," they reply in unison, not bothering to turn away

from the TV as it blares on.

"I need you guys to stop leaving your stuff in the driveway. One of these days I'm not going to see it and kersplat!, it will be squashed and ready for the trash."

"Ok," they reply together.

"Where's your mom?" Karl asks.

"In the kitchen," again in unison, and again focused entirely on the screen.

With a smirk, Karl wanders into the kitchen and finds Kathy there leaning against the counter, staring into space. He watches her for a moment, gathering his courage.

"What's wrong?" he asks with trepidation, wondering what he might have done to evoke such a state from his wife.

After a hesitation, she snaps out of her trance, reads the concern on Karl's face, gives him a smile, and says, "Don't worry, it isn't anything you've done. I just had a rough day, and I was going through it in my head. It started with me running late dropping the kids at school, and then I found Kyle's lunch box still in the car when I stopped for gas after dropping them off, so I had to run it back out to the school. That made me late for my doctor's appointment. For some reason, doctors seem to think people enjoy just sitting around, because they left me in the lobby waiting room for forty-five minutes, and then they moved me to the examination room where I waited for another thirty minutes before the doctor came in. Maybe they were punishing me for being late. By the time I got out of there the morning was gone, so I hurried home to pick up the kitchen and start making a dent in the laundry that's been piling up. That's when I found the message from Mom. With all the rushing around, I totally forgot that I was supposed to meet her for lunch. Next thing I know, it's time to pick up the kids, and the day has gone by. I feel like I didn't really get anything done except a lot of rushing around."

Karl waits patiently for his wife to finish, then, relieved that he's not the cause of her frazzled state, he offers a suggestion. "You know, your birthday is coming up. Maybe your gift can be something to help you organize your days better. Maybe an iPad or something, with a calendar, alerts, to-do lists—"

Kathy's cold, silent stare halts Karl in midsentence. "Don't you think I know about iPads? My phone can do all the things you're talking about! I don't need an iPad, and I'm not looking for solutions from you right now. It's called venting, and I just want you to listen and be sympathetic for a few minutes!" she says.

"Ok," Karl replies.

Unsure what more to say, Karl simply does what she said; he listens. But Kathy only stares back.

"Well, aren't you going to say anything?" Kathy asks.

"But I'm listening!" Karl says.

"Aaarrrggh!" Kathy exclaims and storms off.

As Karl watches her go, he imagines how much better the last twenty seconds would have gone if Kathy had a teleprompter attached to her forehead for him to follow.

Men and women have been sharing this world for more than a million years, yet men don't appear to understand women any better now than they did when loincloths were in fashion and dating consisted of three grunts and the swing of a club. The previous section (A man doesn't think like a woman) contains many topics and examples that might give men a better understanding of how women perceive men, but there are a few additional items that men should take into consideration about the inner workings of their female counterpart.

All women want to feel smart, successful, capable, and independent, but they also at times want to feel that they are being protected and cared for. We recognize that we are treading on dangerously politically incorrect territory here, but let's go with it for now.

Why is it that the vast majority of women would never consider dating a man shorter than they? In modern society a shorter man has equal opportunity for the success and financial security that provides a stable and comfortable home life, and he can certainly have a lean build, an attractive face, and a lustrous head of hair. Yet, a short man will most likely end up with an even shorter woman. Could it be that women, regardless of their drive for career success and independence, have an innate – perhaps even instinctive – need to feel protected and safe, and therefore seek out a man who is larger and more imposing than themselves? A man who – according to that primitive part of the woman's brain – will protect her from sabretooth tigers and handily bring down even the largest, most fierce woolly mammoth.

Women are often more complex than men in many ways.

There is no denying that women are more complex creatures than men. They often have emotions, feelings, and needs that conflict with one another. Independent yet protected. Capable yet cared for. This presents a challenge for a man, particularly considering he is a linear, analytical thinker. Just as there is a need for women to understand how men think, men must also learn to understand how women think, and respond to their needs if a life-long harmonious relationship is to be achieved. While the contrast may present some challenges, it's also what makes marriage exciting and interesting. A man and a woman go together like two jigsaw puzzle pieces. You might have to turn the pieces several times before they snap into place.

Because women are complex creatures, it is difficult to formulate hard and fast rules for how men interact with them, but here are some basic guidelines that we believe are fairly universal:

Sometimes women just need to vent.

- Resist your male instinct to immediately try to solve all problems. Just because you are a hammer, that does not mean every one of your woman's venting sessions are nails.

- Listen attentively, empathetically, and actively. You need to give her 100% of your attention, which means turning off the TV, turning away from the computer, putting down the phone, and making eye contact.

- Wait until she finishes, without interrupting, and then ask her if there is anything you can do to help; don't give unsolicited advice or solutions.

- This is an excellent opportunity to learn and apply new skills in the areas of *acknowledging* and *validating*. The two parts to this skill are telling your wife that you understand her feelings (acknowledge), and that most people would feel the same way in her situation (validate). Sounds simple, but it is powerful!

Women have different ideas about modesty.

- Men may be perfectly happy walking around the house naked, but opening the bedroom curtains while your wife is half-dressed will always lead to trouble.

Though a patient wife won't object to an occasional discrete *boob grab,* **there is a time and place for everything.**

- Not when the kids might sneak up on you at any moment.

- Not when she's upset and/or trying to vent.

- Not when she's on the phone with her father. Well…maybe then.

When it comes to a night on the town, **women have a different definition for getting dressed up.**

- Don't be surprised if your woman expects you to wear socks for that special occasion.

- Use common sense. If she's wearing a cocktail dress, then jeans are definitely out! Don't even ask!

- While dressing-up may be painful, just think how fun it will be to take that fancy dress off your wife when the evening is over. And, if she's wearing a fancy dress, she's also wearing makeup, if you can get to her in time.

- Although you may dread it, your wife looks for opportunities to dress up and go out. For the good of your relationship, give this to her.

Before choosing a movie for the two of you to watch, remember:

- No matter how much you think it's a classic film, seeing *Rambo* for the tenth time is not what she has in mind. Even though she may not mind a good action movie once in a while, she's not a guy.

- She probably doesn't expect you to suffer through *The Devine Secrets of the Traveling Ya-Ya Magnolia Pants*. Conversely, if the movie you have in mind contains bodily dismemberment, more than a dozen explosions, or a double-digit body count, she probably won't enjoy it as much as you think she will.

- Before leaving the house, discuss, compromise, and agree on a type of movie that you can both enjoy.

The most cherished acts of giving are those that require sacrifice on the part of the giver. Without recognizing and embracing the differences between men and women, it is impossible for the giver to make those sacrifices, and less likely that the receiver will appreciate them.

> *The most cherished acts of giving are those that require sacrifice.*

Giving is not restricted to material items, but includes those little things that may seem insignificant: breakfast in bed for your sick spouse; succumbing to your spouse's seductive advances even though you're ready for sleep; offering to watch your spouse's favorite movie without prompting.

Once you become hooked on the pleasure that comes from giving to your spouse, you will look for every opportunity to do so. What's more satisfying than doing nice things for your spouse for selfish reasons, not to mention the fringe benefits that come from a pleasantly surprised mate?

A Man Never Stops Being a Man

Kathy arrives home after a fun Happy Hour outing with her girlfriends. She walks into the house and heads straight for the boys' room, gratefully finding that Karl has already put them to bed, and she gets the rare pleasure of calmly getting herself ready for a restful night's sleep.

Walking into the bedroom, she finds Karl lying in bed attentively watching the television.

"Hi Honey. How was your night out with the girls?" Karl asks.

"It was fun, but I'm exhausted. Thanks for getting the kids to bed on schedule." She glances at the television and says, "What on earth are you watching?"

"Can you believe it? It's a re-run of one of the Victoria's Secret Fashion Shows."

After a brief silence, Kathy replies, "Oh. Is that the only thing you could find to watch?"

"There are other shows on, but nothing quite as *interesting* as this," he quips, waggling his eyebrows.

"Is that so?" Kathy says, and then brusquely turns toward the bathroom to get ready for bed. Ignorant of the tension in the air, Karl waits in bed watching the parade of scantily clad women on the screen.

Several minutes later Kathy emerges from the bathroom, makeup removed and pajamas in place. "Are you still watching this?" Kathy asks as she climbs into the bed.

"Oh, you should have seen the outfit the last girl was wearing. It's probably illegal in most countries," and then he laughs at his own joke.

Kathy crosses her arms and says, "What makes you think I'd want to see that? I can't understand why *you're* watching it. What I see is a lot of silicone and Botox on parade. Do you find them more attractive than me, is that why you're watching it?"

Finally realizing his predicament, he says, "No! Of course not! They're ugly! You're beautiful!"

"Well, I must not be that beautiful if you feel like you need to watch this," she fires back.

Karl quickly turns off the television, and as the *discussion* continues, without a good ending in sight, he eventually decides that his best defense is to pretend to fall asleep, knowing that a cold shoulder will most likely be waiting for him in the morning. *Tomorrow is another day*, he kids himself, *she'll probably forget all about this by then.*

Men are pigs! That is the message our society has been espousing and embracing for decades now. As this mentality has gradually been inserted into the minds of many women and girls, the definition of what makes men pigs has evolved. Men that cheat on their wives are certainly pigs, and anyone other than a cheating husband would very likely agree. The same is true of men that are infatuated with pornography. But evolution of the man-pig has gone too far when men are expected to stop being men.

Just as most women drool over the latest Hollywood hunk, men are going to drool over a beautiful woman. After all, saying

"I do" does not activate a hidden switch in the man's libido that magically makes all other women appear ugly to his eyes. Noticing other women doesn't mean a man is going to cheat on his wife, or that he does not find his wife beautiful and desirable. Unless your man has given specific cause to not trust him, you need to allow him the trust he has worked so hard to earn. Give him credit for marrying you for more than just your good looks. You have qualities and values that make you attractive to him, and that means you can relax. Just because he voices that the woman in the Victoria's Secret ad is attractive doesn't mean he is going to jump through the television to get to her. A rose might be a particular woman's favorite flower, but it doesn't mean she can't admire tulips, lilies, and azaleas. A smart man knows how to be more subtle when admiring other *flowers*, but admire he does. Indeed, he treasures and respects his own rose, not just its visual beauty, but all of its qualities, while also keeping in mind her thorns.

Humans have a more complicated mating ritual when compared to any other creature on Earth. Nearly all other species are either monogamous or polygamous by instinctive drive. Humankind is at a slight disadvantage in this department since we don't have instinct to completely guide us. Like other creatures, we may have the instinctive urge to procreate, but must rely on reason rather than instinct to guide the decisions made before and after the act itself. There are emotional, moral, religious, and social components that help us stay on track. People that are genuinely in love will not usually have a problem maintaining exclusivity, particularly when accompanied by the commitment of marital vows, and the sense of family that comes with it.

Being civilized creatures, we also have societal rules by which we must live, which include honoring commitments. Very few people view infidelity as acceptable behavior. Generally, most people want to remain in our modern "tribal community" and so avoid behavior that threatens their standing or status. Maintaining a loving, trusting, and faithful relationship requires work, perseverance, and strong will for our intricate species.

It takes time and effort to earn a person's trust. In most relationships, this accomplishment takes place before the wedding bells ring, and if not, the relationship is off to a very rocky start. There are also those that hear the wedding bells like a starter's pistol signaling their launch into jealousy and distrust. For them, the dating and engagement periods posed no threat, but now that they're married, they feel

> *Love, trust, and faithfulness require effort and strong will.*

that they possess the other person and *everyone else better keep their paws off!*

Possessiveness and misplaced distrust can threaten what is otherwise a good relationship. Finding the cause or origin of these feelings is crucial to overcoming them. Problematic past relationships, issues within one's family of origin, and the promiscuity that runs rampant in modern society could all lead to unwarranted distrust of one's spouse. Identifying the root cause of your insecurities and resisting the tendency to project those outside problems onto your spouse may help you overcome any misplaced worries about infidelity. If necessary, you may need to seek counseling to overcome these unresolved issues and learn how to trust once again. Trust is a cornerstone of every good, solid, and lifelong marriage.

As we saw with Karl and Kathy, thinking that you are the only person on earth that your spouse finds physically attractive will invariably lead to trouble. There will always be other beautiful women and other handsome men. Accepting this reality and feeling the freedom to discuss it without insecurity or suspicion helps couples avoid the sporadic outbursts over minor comments or actions.

In our own marriage, we use "The List" to accomplish this task in a fun, non-threatening, way. This is a simple game where each spouse comes up with a list of the five celebrities or famous people that they think are the most attractive in the world. You cannot personally know the five people, and the possibility of ever meeting them must be extremely remote, however, fantasizing about them is fair game.

Once you both have your lists complete, share your lists with one another, but do not give specifics on why a particular person is on your list. Likewise, never ask your partner why someone is on their list, and don't criticize or doubt their choices. Keep your list updated and share with your spouse whenever you have replaced someone on the list with another celebrity. Remember, you can only have five people on the list at any one time! Done correctly, this game can help desensitize a couple from the insecurities brought on by innocent comments about the opposite sex.

A good, observant husband knows how to please his wife, as well as how to stay under the radar of her wrath. He tries to avoid doing stupid things that tend to make her angry. But at the same time, he cannot help being a man, as he should be, and as his wife should want him to be. The wife needs to understand that her husband is *wired* differently, and she must embrace these differences, respect him as a partner, and understand that he can faithfully love her beyond measure, even while not being blind to the fact that there are other beautiful women in the world.

A Woman Never Stops Being a Woman

It's Friday night, and Karl and Kathy are snuggling on the couch watching an old, classic, romantic movie that Karl picked up on his way home from work.

This particular movie wouldn't be Karl's first choice – not even his hundredth choice, or thousandth for that matter – but he specifically chose this type of movie in an attempt to make brownie points with his wife, knowing how much she loves them. After all, you can never have too many brownie points.

The kids are quietly tucked in bed, popcorn is made, wine is poured, and their special TV watching blanket is in place. It's finally the *adult moment* they've been waiting for all week. The adult moment to which all parents of young children look forward. Kathy rests her head on Karl's shoulder as the movie plays, the blue light from the screen washing over them in the darkened living room, the television on low volume.

On the screen, in splendid black and white, a stylishly groomed man pilots a topless two-seater sports car through the cobblestone streets of a European town, an impeccably dressed woman beside him in the passenger seat. The car pulls to the curb in front of a restaurant, the man quickly hops out and jogs to the passenger door, tossing the car keys to the awaiting uniformed valet in the process, and opens the car door for his lady companion, offering his hand to assist her in exiting the low-slung vehicle. She then hooks her arm in his, and he proceeds to escort her inside the swanky-looking restaurant.

"Those were the days," Kathy says to Karl with a sigh.

"Yeah," Karl says. "It seems like things were just so much simpler then. A more relaxed pace."

"Sometimes I feel like I was born in the wrong era. I'd really fit in back then."

"I know what you mean," Karl says. "They wore some really cool clothes back then."

"Right?" Kathy says. "Even for a simple evening on the town, people dressed for the occasion."

"And those old sports cars are awesome. It seems like everyone drives convertible sports cars in these old movies," Karl says.

Kathy lifts her head from Karl's shoulder and turns to face him. "And the men were such gentlemen. So dashing! The way he opened the door for her and helped her out of the car. I remember when you used to open the car door for me back when we were dating," she says to him, teasingly, touching the end of his nose.

"Yeah, it's nice not having to worry about *that* anymore," Karl jokingly replies.

"I didn't realize being a gentleman was such a chore."

"Well, it's not that it's such a chore," Karl says. "It's just that we've been married for ten years."

"So, I guess you feel you don't need to impress me anymore," she says, a little coolness creeping into her voice. "You don't need to work at it. Is that what you're saying?"

"I just thought women didn't like that kind of stuff anymore," Karl says.

"What does that mean? Do you think I don't want to be treated like a lady anymore?" Kathy says, all good humor gone from her face and voice. "I'm a modern woman, but you haven't found any of my bras torched, have you?"

"Well, I just thought--"

"How about I let you know when I'm ready for you to start taking me for granted?"

"I never intended to take you for granted." Karl replies.

"Then is it too much to ask that you open a door for me once in a while?"

"I'd love to open doors for you," Karl says, "I didn't realize it was so important to you." Inside his mind he kicks himself thinking, *why did I pick this movie? I should have gone with* Rambo. *I've never seen him open a door for anyone, unless it's with a rocket launcher.*

It's very normal for chivalry to relax some after years of marriage. As a couple becomes comfortable with one another and develops a rhythm, the way they treat each other evolves. Not necessarily devolving from good to bad, but simply evolving into something new.

However, while the couple may become more comfortable like an old pair of jeans, all women still want to be treated with respect. Comfort and good manners are not mutually exclusive, and a man can be very comfortable in his marriage but still practice good manners with this person he loves above all others. During our own years of marriage, we have witnessed firsthand many couples where the

> *Chivalry tends to relax, but should not disappear.*

man no longer opens doors for his wife, yet that same man will gladly, even eagerly, open the door for an older person, a young child, or a woman he does not know. Unfortunately, most men that have slid into this mode of behavior will not change their course until they are *called on the carpet* by their wife and made to feel like a worm.

If your manners have slipped, your wife has probably noticed even if she hasn't said anything to you about it. Rather than wait for the sting of the whip, heed the pull of the carrot. Take an inventory yourself and make the necessary changes. Brownie points await you for the effort.

We are using the opening of doors as an example, but there are many things a man should continue doing for his mate throughout dating and marriage (*hint: they should be done without being asked*):

- Lifting/carrying heavy objects (even if they aren't really all that heavy).
- Reaching for high objects.
- Opening that tight lid on the jar of pickles.
- Offering your jacket on a cool evening.
- Opening the car door for special occasions *at a minimum* (if she's wearing a dress, open the door!), and opening all other doors every time.
- Being a gentleman reaches beyond the marriage; your wife will respect and admire you all the more if you take time to help an older woman carry her groceries to her car at the store, help a woman change a flat tire, give up your seat for the elderly, pregnant, or disabled when using public transportation.

This is not a comprehensive list but gives a few ideas on how a husband can also be a gentleman. Done proactively, you will immediately harvest the fruits of your labors in the form of smiles, hugs, kisses, and who knows what else.

Chivalry can make a man feel manly. By performing these chivalrous acts, the man's place in the relationship is demonstrated, as is the role of the woman. Just as the man wants to feel manly, most women want to feel feminine. However, feeling feminine is not the same as being inferior or subordinate to the man. Each participant in the relationship brings their own strengths and abilities for the betterment of the marriage and the family. A wife is a partner to her husband, and as a partner her opinion, input, desires, and ideas are every bit as valuable and relevant as his. Make sure your wife feels important to you and to the marriage, accomplishing this through actions and words.

Another important reason for keeping chivalry alive in a marriage is the children. Once those little ones come along and begin soaking up all that they see and hear, everything the parents do is an opportunity to demonstrate what a good marriage looks like. A boy is closely watching the father to see how to behave like a gentleman, as well as how a man should treat the woman he loves. He's also watching the mother to see how she responds to being treated in that way. A girl is watching the father to see how she should be treated by the opposite sex, and she's watching the mother to see how she should conduct herself in the face of chivalry (or the lack

Treating your wife with respect shows her how important she is to you.

thereof), and what to expect from the man she loves.

Although chivalry represents the courtesy a man shows a woman, it is really a two-way arrangement. Out of chivalry, a man will hold a door open for a lady he doesn't know, which demonstrates that it is not something that is earned by the woman. However, if a woman does not show appreciation to her man for continued chivalrous treatment, it communicates to the man that he doesn't need to do it anymore. Chivalry will survive when it is demonstrated continuously and appreciated just as frequently.

Embracing Differences

Men and women are different. Thank God! Imagine how boring life would be if we were the same. But different doesn't mean inferior, it doesn't mean incorrect, and it certainly doesn't mean subordinate. Different simply means that the other person brings something to the table that you may not possess, something that you may need and value without even realizing it. Keeping those differences intact maintains a balance and keeps marriage interesting.

Putting those differences to work for your relationship and household will not only be advantageous to productivity, but will also strengthen the respect and admiration you and your spouse have for one another.

It is not a lack of love, but a lack of
friendship that makes unhappy
marriages.
- Friedrich Nietzsche

5

Home, Sweet, Safe, Supportive Home

Those first one or two years of marriage are truly bliss. Each day you watch the clock at work, waiting for five o'clock to roll around so you can get home. Dinners are frequently eaten out, so it's almost as if you're still dating. There is still some impressing to do, so you're still nice to one another, using manners, praising one another for the littlest things, relishing gifts received, and constantly trying to please the other while stroking each other's ego.

Fast forward ten years. The marriage is not on the verge of collapse, but the bliss has turned to blisters, and the quiet life of a young married couple has become the insanity known as a young family. Work, school, extracurricular activities, keeping groceries in the refrigerator, laundry for the troops, and all the other grind leaves little time to think straight. The relationship is mostly strong, but it has reached a "comfort zone" where both parties are comfortable in the routine, and there is little room for excitement. In this environment, it's difficult for a husband or wife to recognize how important the other person is in their life, or to feel that the other person appreciates them like they once did.

Daily chores are not the only culprits potentially putting a wedge between man and wife. Once the children come, they need an incredible amount of love and attention to flourish and grow into the kind of people we all want our children to be. But even in this area, there must be some balance. Give love and support unconditionally to your children, but don't forget that you have a spouse that also still needs your love and support. A lack of balance in this regard can result in one's spouse feeling like they are playing a secondary role in the family, and this affects not only the couple, but the children can also come to feel that they are the *center* of the family, rather than *members* of a family. Left unchecked, this situation can be a marriage killer once the children are grown and gone. The empty nest is not only empty of the chicks, but is also empty of a loving and close marriage, with two strangers trying to figure out what happened.

Everyone wants to feel important, appreciated, and needed.

Human beings have a natural need to feel important, appreciated, and needed by others, and their mental, emotional, and psychological health is directly impacted by this need; positively when it is met, and negatively when it is not. Two possible scenarios can result when this requirement goes unful-filled: the person will look to fulfill the need elsewhere, or the person will gradually spiral down the vortex of low self-esteem. Either of these scenarios can lead to trouble for the relationship, as the former could take the shape of an extra-marital affair, long work hours, or excessive time on the golf course, and the latter could become a pattern of detachment, indifference, and even depression.

Your spouse is the most important person in your life, and you must make a conscious effort to recognize the vital role that person plays in your world and find ways to show your appreciation for the value they bring to the household and your relationship.

Make Your Man Feel Important

Karl just finished one of the worst days he can remember. He arrived at work a little late, only to be immediately chewed-out by his boss for a mistake he'd made on a contract he had typed up the day before which – had it not been spotted – would have cost the company a bundle of money. And as fate would have it, today was his annual review, upon which his next raise – or lack thereof – is based. He had been working hard for the past year, putting in what he felt was some of his very best work, but now he wondered how much that one little mistake at the penultimate moment will cost him.

As if that wasn't enough, at lunch he managed to squirt ketchup all over the front of his white shirt and, considering his annual review meeting was to take place immediately after lunch, he did not have time to go home to change. In the process of removing the above-mentioned stain, he only managed to spread it over a larger area of the shirt, the stain now looking a bit like a pink map of Texas.

Somehow, he survived it all, and annual review done, work day finished, and rush hour traffic behind him, Karl has finally made it home to his sanctuary.

"I'm so glad you're home! You won't believe the day I had," Kathy says to Karl as he walks through the door. Without hesitating, she goes on, "They called me from the school because Kyle was sick, and so I had to cancel lunch with my friends. It turned into a day of cleaning up after Kyle, which means I didn't get any of the errands done that were on my list. And by the way, Kirk has been waiting for you upstairs. You're supposed to help him with his science project."

"I didn't exactly have a great day either," Karl responds. "You know that contract I've been--"

"You don't know how lucky you are to be in a nice office all day with peace and quiet. I wish we could trade places sometimes," Kathy says.

"Yeah, me too. You wouldn't believe--"

"You better hurry upstairs and help Kirk, because dinner will be ready in just a little while."

"Can I just take time to change out of my suit before I go up?"

Kathy responds with a roll of her eyes.

It's obvious from Kathy's comments and verbal tone that she doesn't respect Karl's role in the family, nor the job he performs outside the house. If it's obvious to us, it's obvious to Karl, as well. After years of this treatment, Karl's self-esteem and motivation will surely suffer, which will be reflected in his limited career growth and salary potential. Or Karl can take another course of action, which is comprised of progressively longer hours at work in a subconscious effort to avoid the disrespectful atmosphere at home. This second path will be great for Karl's career, but devastating to his marriage and to his role as a father. Either of these scenarios reveals that Kathy's attitude and behavior relative to Karl's family role results in a self-destructive outcome for both of them.

Why is Kathy reacting in this way to Karl? Fifty years ago, women's and men's roles were clearly defined, but women were often not given the proper level of respect for their capabilities and the role they performed at home. In the workplace, for those that worked, they went largely underappreciated by their male counterparts. That situation needed to change. However, the pendulum has swung too far the other direction in some cases. In an effort to accelerate the balancing of the gender gap, two strategies were employed simultaneously. Strategy one was a conscious legal, societal, and political push for equal rights, equal pay, equal opportunity, and equal respect between men and women. This was a sound strategy and very much overdue. Unfortunately, the other subtle – even subliminal – strategy was to make men look stupid, incompetent, and inferior to women in order to achieve that acceleration of change.

If you look at children's programming over the past decade or two, in almost all cases the primary female character is smarter, craftier, and even physically stronger than the male character. The male character is usually the bumbling, slow-witted sidekick. This attitude is also reflected in our female-dominated elementary school system, where girls are often generally considered *good* and boys *bad*. As each successive generation of self-esteem deprived boys become men and have their own children, what will become of the male gender?

In the face of this move to emasculate the males of our society, what has happened to the expectations of most women? Simply put, they want a bipolar man. But rather than manic/depressive, they are looking for a man who can instantly change from strong, powerful, rugged, assertive, and confident to sweet, tender, caring, attentive, sensitive, and even servile. They want equal parts gladiator and effeminate cabana boy. The fact that this type of man doesn't really exist is causing great frustration for many women.

As we've made clear throughout this book, men and women are programmed differently at a fundamental level. This in no way implies that one is better than the other, but simply that they have different strengths to contribute to the team, and expectations need to be set accordingly. In an earlier chapter, we discussed how roles can impact a marriage. Let's look at another way this encounter between husband and wife could have gone when each of them respects the other person's role, and with them using words and actions to let one another know how important they are to the family.

Men and women have different strengths to contribute to the team.

On the other side of the neighborhood from Karl and Kathy, Jack walks into his house after an exceptionally hectic day, and Jill asks him, "How was your day?"

"Horrible. After I settle in a little, I'd like to tell you about it," knowing that immediately dumping on his wife might make him feel better, but she may not be ready for it just yet.

Jill gives Jack a hug and says, "Sorry to hear that, Honey. I'm so glad you're home. My day didn't go so well, either, and it'll be good to vent a little. I'll tell you what, why don't you get comfy, and when you're ready, Joey needs help with that science project. Maybe it'll be good for you to put your mind on something else for a while, and you are the resident science guy of this house. After dinner, we'll put the boys to bed, share some horror stories, and then we can *console* each other. Hint, hint."

Later that evening, when all is quiet in the house, they share their days' stories, and when Jack is finished, Jill says, "I wouldn't worry about it. You've been doing a great job, and if they have any brains, they'll recognize how valuable you are to the company. You know how valuable you are to me and the kids. If I was your boss, I'd give you a big raise," and she chuckles and nuzzles him.

"Well, I'm sorry I couldn't help out today with Jimmy. I know how stressful it is taking care of them when they're sick. It sounds like half the class went home sick. Maybe you can get together with Kathy and your other friends for a drink tomorrow evening since you missed out on lunch today. I'll take the boys out for a bite, assuming Jimmy's up to it by then."

"We rescheduled the lunch for Friday, but that was sweet of you."

"Of course," Jack replies. "So, when does that real *consoling* begin?"

Through this interaction, Jack felt appreciated, important, and loved. By getting this level of support, he can empathize with his wife and return the support in a loving way, creating a feeling of unity. Here are some other things women can do to ensure their husbands feel needed and important:

- Ask him to open a tightly sealed jar for you (even if maybe you can do it yourself)
- Ask him to carry heavy objects for you
- Recognize and thank him when he does things for you, especially if he does them without prompting, and even if he didn't do it quite the way you would, while withholding any critical commentary in your mind
- Compliment him on his looks or on the way he dresses once in a while without waiting for him to fish for the compliment (while, on average, men may not feel as self-conscious about their appearance as women, they still want to be attractive)
- Come up with Neanderthal tasks for him to perform around the house, like doing away with critters that don't belong in the house, remembering that in many ways men often want to act the caveman part
- Value the gifts he gives you, remembering that even if it wasn't exactly what you had in mind, he put time and effort into choosing what he thought was the perfect item

Conversely, here are some things that will make your husband feel unappreciated or disrespected:

- Talking to your husband as if he were one of the children; remember to switch gears from mom-mode to wife-mode
- Forgetting to say please and thank you; the more you say these things, the more often he'll give you reason to say them
- Negatively comparing your husband to other husbands, whether he's present or not (and not even in your thoughts to the extent it can be avoided); focus on the valuable attributes your husband has

- Quashing your husband's judgment, opinion, or ideas for the sake of someone else's; he will not always be right, but don't assume someone else's views (your parents', friends', or coworkers') will always have more merit than his; sometimes he will be flat-out wrong, but be gentle.

Self-esteem is near the top of the Hierarchy of Needs pyramid for a reason, and feeling important in the eyes of the people we love has a large impact on one's self-esteem. When one's needs are met at home, one doesn't look outside the home for fulfillment. It is not unusual for the soothing, reassuring words and actions from one spouse to another to diminish with the passing years of marriage, but a conscious effort must be made to retain and rejuvenate the value a couple sees in one another, restoring the feelings that were more prevalent when the relationship was new.

Make Your Woman Feel Important

Once again, men can learn many things from the previous section, particularly in the area of nurturing your spouse's self-esteem. Many of the tactics are the same for a husband that wants to make his wife feel important, but there are some differences that need to be addressed. Take into consideration the following scenario:

Jack arrives home after work on a Friday and finds Jill sitting at her kitchen desk staring at her computer screen. He can tell by her face that she's not in a good mood.

"What's up, honey?" he asks.

"Oh, I'm just sitting here remembering the days when I was *somebody*." She responds in a dramatic voice.

"Okay. Let 'er rip. What happened?" Jack asks.

"No, you just got home. Relax for a little while and we can talk later."

"Actually, I had a pretty good day, so let's tackle this while it's fresh," Jack says, as he grabs two wine glasses from the cupboard and a bottle of wine from the refrigerator, pours two healthy servings, hands one of the glasses to Jill, then settles against the counter to listen.

Jill explains how her friend Beth, who still works in the office Jill had worked in before becoming a stay-home-mom, just got a huge promotion accompanied by a big office and a big raise. Beth had called all excited about it, not meaning to brag, but coming across as bragging nonetheless.

"I trained her!" Jill says in frustration. "I would have gotten that promotion if I was still there and she knows it. But I made the choice to stay here to raise my children because I thought it was important. Though, sometimes I wonder if anyone really appreciates what I do here. The other day Joey asked me what I do all day while he's at school. But he wasn't asking because he was curious. I could tell from his tone that he thinks I don't do anything all day, or just spend all my time goofing off. He stressed the last *do*. As in, 'what do you *do* all day?'"

"Okay, okay, okay. Slow down. Breathe," Jack says. "Let's keep in mind that Joey is in grade school. In his mind, he's picturing what he'd do all day if *he* didn't have to go to school. No doubt, he'd goof around all day, so he assumes that's what you do. But me, on the other hand, I'm not in grade school, and I know what you do all day. I wouldn't trade jobs with you even if there was a seven-figure salary involved. I don't know how you keep that many balls in the air at one time."

"You're just trying to make me feel better," Jill says, beginning to unwind. "Let's face it, when was the last time a promotion was handed out for outstanding achievement in laundry processing?"

"I know that your job seems thankless most of the time, but the fact is, the boys and I would be lost without you. Running the house does not only include the routine tasks you do, such as the laundry. You're shaping our kids' lives to make them the young men they're going to become. Somehow, I don't think Beth will be lying on her deathbed in fifty years saying, 'If only I had spent more time at work.' She can never get back these years, and before she knows it, her kids will be graduating from high school and she'll wonder where the years went."

"I guess," Jill says, the tension visibly beginning to leave her shoulders.

"And you said she just got a promotion, right? Do you think two months from now anyone will really remember that she had been working in her previous position for five years? No. They'll see the new person doing the job just as well as Beth had done it, and it will be as if Beth had never been there. The same will be true of her new position when she gets promoted again. Is that a legacy?"

"But do you think the kids will ever appreciate what I do and the choices I've made for their benefit?"

"If all goes well," Jack says, "they won't appreciate it for a long time to come. What they have is all they know. They have a clean, secure home, clothes to wear, healthy food to eat, and a mom that is always there for them, night or day, ready to pick them up when they fall, or to wipe their tears away, or even to wipe the snot from their noses. And if you were gone, there's no one that can take your place. No one else is going to touch that snot! They will only have one mom for as long as they live. The only way for them to appreciate what they have is to lose it, which I certainly hope never happens."

"Jeez, I hope not, too!" Jill says, smiling.

"Every time I see one of them do something that I know they learned by watching you, it hits me how much you influence their lives and who they are. You know how you do the sign of the cross whenever you hear an ambulance or fire truck siren? The other day when I was taking the boys to the store with me, an ambulance passed by with lights and siren, and they both crossed themselves. Even Jimmy, and he's only five!"

"Really? I started doing that when I was little after seeing my mom do it," Jill says, with tears glistening in the corners of her eyes.

"When they're adults and they look back at this time, especially when they have their own children, that's when it will hit them how much you and I both have done for them throughout their lives. They might not ever say it, but they'll know."

"Thanks, Jack. I just lose perspective sometimes, and it's good to hear things like that from you. I know we've talked about this multiple times before," Jill says, "but it's good to hear it again, every once in a while, to recharge my confidence in what I do," She stands and gives Jack a hug.

"You have a good reason to feel confident in what you do," Jack says. "You do it well. You create a real home. To me, going home after a long day at work to a house that sat empty all day doesn't feel much like a home. That might sound old-fashioned, but that's the way I feel. I'm sure you'd feel the same way if we were to reverse roles."

"Thanks for the pep talk, coach. Dinner is just about ready, and I think I'm ready to face the next six months of motherhood, at the end of which I'll probably need another one of these talks."

"I'll be ready," Jack replies.

Jill gives Jack one more squeeze, and they turn to the kitchen to get the meal on the table together.

Words are powerful. They can sting and take a person down to the lowest level, or they can encourage, nurture, and build a person up. The right words can make a person feel both important and loved. Speaking from the heart, your words can help your spouse face just about anything, especially with you at their side.

Make Your Spouse Feel Loved

The relationship between a husband and wife is not just very special – it's also completely unique. It's different from any other relationship in their lives, and that singular emotional intimacy between them results in a truly exclusive bond. This is why treating your spouse with the utmost respect and courtesy is so important. It is a demonstration and acknowledgement of that unparalleled relationship.

A couple must share each other with the outside world for most of their waking hours, which is why time must be set aside for them to just be a couple for each other. Although a woman will sometimes make arrangements for this *couple time*, it's important for the man to express his desire for private intimate moments with his wife by also taking the initiative to make the plans for a special evening out. A romantic dinner for two on a regular basis acts as a constant affirmation of the special relationship that exists solely between the two of them. A marriage starts with two lovers and stays strong and exciting when that spark is kept alive.

The unique bond shared by a husband and wife is also reflected in the way they speak to one another, as well as how they speak to others about their spouse. "I love you" has become a bit of a cliché in our modern times. It's very easy to say it, even if you don't mean it, and it's often said out of habit. Of course, we should tell our spouse that we love him or her daily, but that simply isn't enough. What we say to other people about our spouse, and how we say it, is a very powerful way of expressing our true feelings. Take the following conversation, for example:

Jack and Jill are out having dinner with some other couples. Their new friends, Martin and Maria, arrived a while ago, and the four of them are already halfway through their first glass of wine, nibbling on appetizers, and getting better acquainted. They are waiting for Karl and Kathy to arrive before ordering entrees.

A few minutes later Karl and Kathy hurry into the restaurant and spot the rest of the group across the room. They get seated, and after introductions and the usual pleasantries, Karl apologizes for their lateness, saying, "We could have been on time, but Kathy had to try on every dress in her closet before finally settling on the first one she had tried on." He says this kiddingly, but it's clear to all present that the ride to the restaurant might have been uncomfortable.

Kathy just smiles sheepishly.

"Oh, I know exactly what Kathy was going through," Maria says, in fellowship with her female comrade. "That happens to me all the time, where I just don't like the way any of my clothes look on me."

"I told her the first dress she tried on looked fine," Karl says. "She acts as if she's getting ready for the Miss America pageant or something every time we go out."

"I don't mind so much when Maria goes through that, since I get to sit and watch her change clothes for twenty minutes," Martin says teasingly, knowing he's embarrassing his wife a little. "There are certainly worse things than seeing my wife in nothing but her underwear over and over again. She always looks great in the first thing she tries on, but no way I'm telling her that until we're at least five or six outfits into the process."

"Maaartin!" Maria playfully berates him.

"What are you guys, newlyweds or something?" Jack asks.

"No, not by a long shot," Martin says. "We're about to celebrate our fifteenth anniversary next month. It's hard to believe it's already been that long!"

"We just celebrated our tenth anniversary a couple months ago, and went on a great cruise," Kathy says.

"Yeah, I knew that's what Kathy really wanted to do, and I wanted it to be special for her," Karl says. "It was a lot of fun, but I still can't get over how expensive cruises are."

"I thought you wanted to go on the cruise, too," Kathy says. "I didn't realize you were just doing it for me. It was *our* anniversary, not *my* anniversary. We could have done something else."

"The cruise was fine, but I would have been perfectly happy just driving down to the lake for a few days," Karl says. "These guys know what I mean," he continues, looking at the other men at the table. They just stare back noncommittally.

"Fishing? On our tenth anniversary?" Kathy asks.

"Boy a cruise sounds really nice," Maria chimes in. "We've been saving up to take a trip to Hawaii to celebrate our anniversary, and we decided to stay in the same hotel we stayed in for our honeymoon."

"That's so romantic," Jill says. "Jack, I hope you're taking notes. Our anniversary will be here before you know it," she says, wiggling her eyebrows at him.

"I thought about staying in a much nicer hotel this time, since we certainly can afford a better place now that we're 'real adults' with 'real jobs'," Martin says with air quotes. "But we both thought it will be nice to stay in the same place and relive some memories from our honeymoon. I even requested the exact same room to complete the experience."

Jack gently elbows Martin in the ribs, saying, "Hey buddy, you're making the rest of us guys look bad."

"Where did you find this guy?" Kathy asks Maria, "and are there any more like him back home?"

"I guess I just got lucky," Maria replies with a grin.

"Well, cheers to all of us for happy anniversaries, whenever they may be!" Jack says, raising his glass.

Although Karl never says anything specifically derogatory about his wife, he's not putting her or their relationship in the best light. He makes his wife sound difficult and a bit shallow in this public forum, while at the same time making himself sound like an ass.

Martin, on the other hand, by offering just a few honest, heartfelt comments about his wife and marriage has made it clear to both his wife and the other couples present that he is happy in his relationship, and clearly loves his wife. Even more significantly, through Martin's thoughtfulness and consideration, it comes across clearly to Maria that she is important to him.

Showing kindness, respect, and love for our spouse through how we speak about them goes beyond making them feel loved and important. Most of us have very few people in the world who we feel we can trust completely. Your spouse should be at the top of that list. A strong marriage should look a lot like a comic book crime-fighting duo. They will always have each other's back through thick and thin, are there to pick the other one up when they fall down, are always on each other's side, and certainly wouldn't be bad-mouthing their partner to the other spandex-clad warriors at the weekly Friday night mixer. How you speak about your partner can either shatter or build that feeling of trust between you.

The nature of one's marriage relationship is also demonstrated when out in the world without one's spouse. Just as doing the right thing even when nobody is looking is the true test of integrity, saying nice things about one's spouse when they aren't present reveals how one truly feels about that person.

Conversely, as mentioned in an earlier chapter, criticism – and its companion, negativism – can be an escalating process, and left unchecked can result in disdain, discontent, and all too often, divorce. It's possible for someone to love their mate but still have the bad habit of saying not-so-nice things about them to others, leading them down this dangerous path. In changing this behavior, talking about only the good attributes that your spouse possesses, not only will other people have a better opinion of your better-half and admire your relationship, but you will also reap the benefit of continuously reminding yourself why you love this person.

Let's look at this from another angle. It makes sense that what a person says is usually a reflection of what they feel. But what they say can also *more strongly become* what they feel when repeated regularly. This is true of people who look at themselves in the mirror each morning and repeat the mantra "there's nothing I can't do" as they try to boost their own self-confidence, and it's true of a person who continuously disparages their spouse in front of other people.

> Show your love by speaking well of your spouse to others.

If a marriage has hit rocky ground due to spiraling negativism, remembering what we loved about that other person, and speaking of it to that person and others, can help renew the way those attributes made us feel early on in the relationship. Taking some liberties with a well-worn adage, "If you don't have something nice to say, say something nice anyway."

Let's take this one step further for our male readers. Most people would agree that – on average – men are simply not as emotionally light on their feet as women. Improvising on topics of emotions, feelings, relationships, and love is just not in most male genetic code, and what sounded simple and sincere while bouncing around inside their skulls might come out sounding like the exact opposite. That being the case, men will need to do some extra homework in advance to pull off speaking eloquently of their wives' qualities and attributes, whether to her or to other people.

Though primarily directed at men, the following exercise could be beneficial to both husbands and wives. When you have some quiet time to think, come up with the five or six attributes you love most about your spouse. If you have poor short-term memory, write them down on a small piece of paper and put them in a safe place to study later. You will need to memorize them since reading them from the paper will destroy the magic of the moment, and most likely backfire in an ugly way.

Men, once you have become adept at communicating these virtues, you can try some improvisation and extemporaneous speaking. In the previous dialog, Martin was improvising, and doing it beautifully. Make note, though, that you need to speak from your heart with honesty, otherwise it defeats the purpose of saying anything in the first place. Also, steer clear of general platitudes such as "you're the best", or "you are so nice." Be specific and personal with what you have to say, noting characteristics about their person, personality, or behaviors. Saying the right things at the right time reinforces the special, exclusive relationship you share.

The Power of Words

In most work environments, there is opportunity to be praised and rewarded for work well done. It might be a special award accompanied by the requisite plaque, or it may just be the annual merit process, but the recognition and the adjoining satisfaction are there. There is no such system for parenthood, and furthermore, in many ways our modern society sends the message to parents that they are achieving nothing if either parent stays home to raise their children. Therefore, the reward system for the thankless job of *parenthood* must come from within, but it can certainly be boosted by thoughtful words of encouragement from one's spouse.

Tell your spouse how they are valued by you and the children, but before doing so, take the time to mentally reflect on all the things they do for their family, and how important they are, before saying a word to them. You must mean what you say, and empty praise will be evident in your tone, so speak with sincerity. There are times for "sweet talk-

> Tell your spouse how and why they are valued by you.

ing", and there are times for words of heart-felt appreciation that provide validation for the other person. Recognizing the difference is a skill that will benefit both of you. And always keep in mind that the two of you are the primary role models for how your children will treat their spouse and their own children. This is part of your legacy, and an excellent demonstration of love.

Let the wife make the husband glad to
come home, and let him make her sorry
to see him leave.
- Martin Luther

6

Keep the Fire Alive

Two cars roll off the assembly line shiny, new, and perfect. Fill up the tank, hop in, and you're ready to hit the road in style. Twenty years later, after a history of minimal maintenance, hard driving, and harsh environmental conditions, one car looks shabby and ready for the junkyard. The other car, in the hands of a car enthusiast, was constantly tuned, polished, gently driven, and garaged every night, and still looks and drives as if it were new. It might look a bit out of style to the younger generation, but because of the excellent care and maintenance it received over the years, it is now a *classic*.

If we want our marriages to become *classics*, we need to be marriage enthusiasts. In the real world, love and attraction are enough to *get* married, but not enough to *be* married. A marriage must be tuned and maintained to keep running like it did when it was new; to keep the old spark plugs sparking. A husband and wife will change on the outside as the years take their toll and the hair grays, and the relationship will naturally mature. However, even in the face of change and maturation, the relationship does not have to lessen, and can even grow in unexpected ways. But both parties must be committed to the scheduled maintenance program for the marriage to become a true *classic*. Furthermore, there are ways to *soup-up* a marriage, turbocharging it for maximum horsepower.

The rest of this chapter offers tips for keeping the marriage-fire alive, and methods for staving off the eroding effect that the passing years can have on a relationship. These ideas are not presented in any particular order and can be mixed-and-matched to fit your relationship. Some of them apply as easily to young marriages as they do to seasoned ones, while others may only apply to those more mature relationships. All of them are meant to keep marriage fresh and fun.

You're Married, Not Dead!

It's Saturday night, and Jack and Jill are out having dinner with Karl, Kathy, Martin, and Maria. They leisurely made their way through appetizers, and their entrees will be arriving any minute. Most of them are already into their second glass of wine, and conversation has slipped into that comfortable rhythm that a glass and a half of wine amongst friends can create. Their voices are raised as they compete with the noise of the popular restaurant.

"How about we go to Reed's to listen to some jazz after dinner?" Jill suggests to the group.

The other couples are game, but Jack says, "Jill, my mom is watching the kids and she's expecting us back home in about an hour."

"Your mom won't mind. Just give her a call and ask her to stay just a little while longer," Jill replies.

"You know she doesn't like last-minute changes," Jack says.

"Oh, come on. You're her favorite son," Jill says. "She's always looking for ways to help you." She leans in close and quietly whispers in his ear, "besides, I'll make it worth your while when we get home," and she gives him a seductive look.

The table remains quiet as the other couples watch the exchange, then Karl asks, "What was that?!"

"What was what?" Jack and Jill reply in unison.

"That look!"

"What look?"

"I don't know what you just said in his ear," Karl says, "but based on that look, I can take a guess. And I'll also guess that we're about to go listen to some jazz." The rest of them laugh at this.

"Ladies and gentlemen," Jack says with flourish, "a man has to do what a man has to do." With that, he takes out his cell phone and makes a production out of dialing.

"I can't believe these crazy kids," Karl jokes, nodding toward Jack and Jill. "After twelve years of marriage they still act like a couple of horny teenagers."

Hanging up the phone, Jack raises his wineglass and says, "A toast...to babysitting grandmothers and to grateful wives."

"Hear, hear!!"

We see it portrayed all the time in movies and on TV: couples that have been married more than a few years stop having sex. In fact, couples that are still having sex after many years of marriage are often disbelieved or made the butt of jokes. This sexless, indifferent route is not a necessary reality. People still like sex and affection after marriage, as evidenced by the prevalence of infidelity in our society. There are many couples that have been married for more than thirty years that still have an active sex life. The problem is that intimacy with one's own spouse may stop being interesting, sometimes as early as the honeymoon in cases of couples that were sexually active together for years before the wedding bells rang. With time and repetition, intimacy can become mechanical and stale. You need to break the routine to rekindle the fire.

> *Break the routine to rekindle the fire.*

In our modern society, the word *intimacy* is often associated exclusively with sex, but intimacy, and even sex, is broader than sexual intercourse. Most people will agree that a passionate kiss is a sexual act, and when done between two people that care for each other, it is an expression of intimacy. Even a whisper in the ear can be very intimate.

When marriages lose steam after several years, it has more to do with a loss of intimacy than it does a loss of sexual drive, and a kiss can become just a kiss. If the equipment is still working properly from a physical perspective, a couple can certainly still be having sex on a regular basis after twenty years or more, but it will not be as enjoyable if the intimacy is gone. Intimacy doesn't just happen; like many things in marriage, it must be done with conscious effort.

You can't just *take* time for intimate moments; you must *make* time for them. Dating is a tool for keeping a marriage interesting and presents an opportunity to *make* time for your marriage. Though many couples have told us that they don't go on dates because of the expense, especially the cost of baby-sitting, there are ways around this obstacle. Free babysitting certainly reduces the cost of dating, but if you don't have relatives in town to lend a hand, what do you do? There are many couples in the same boat as you, and you probably know a few. If you feel a close relationship with one of those couples, and you feel they are trustworthy, perhaps they feel the same way about you. Arrange child swapping once or twice a month for an evening. Babysitting expense solved!

For some couples, child swapping is not an option, so more creativity is needed if one wants to spend some time out of the house with one's spouse. Suck it up and pay for that babysitter, but let the expense for the evening stop there. There are many activities a couple can do that cost next to nothing. Window shopping, a picnic, a walk around the lake, biking, free concerts and other local events, a hot cup of coffee and a long talk, and even running errands together can give you some quality time with your other half. The only key to a successful date is getting time together, no matter what you're doing with that time.

Does a date have to mean leaving the house? Not necessarily. You must redefine *date* to get the most out of your time together as a couple. Some of the best *dates* we've had were while the kids were upstairs asleep, and we were in front of a roaring fire with a bottle of wine. Other fond memories involve a rented movie and pajamas on a comfortable couch with our legs entwined. Time that you have set aside as a couple, just the two of you, is a date. There are no more excuses.

Although intimacy is not limited to sex, sex is certainly an important – and perhaps the most fun – part of being an intimate couple. However, it is in the area of sex that the stereotypical couple can lose steam after just a few years together. Why does this happen?

Imagine you are on a desert island and will only have one food item to eat for every meal for the next year. You get to choose what that one item is going to be, however, regardless of what item is chosen, most people will be tired of that favorite food within a few days. After an entire year eating only that, they will likely reach a point where they'll never want to eat it again if given the choice.

No matter how good the sex is at the beginning of the marriage, without spicing things up occasionally – having a larger menu from which to choose – you're right back on that desert island. If sex is something that happens only on Saturday nights at 8:37pm, in the bedroom, under the covers, lights out, missionary position, and lasts for precisely five minutes and twenty-four seconds (including foreplay), this is going to get old really fast. Some men, and women, might be grateful for a guaranteed once-a-week romp, but this meal will likely grow tiring in no time at all.

There are many ways to make sex more interesting without even a mention of sexual positions. After all, this is not that kind of book. Rather, just like any *project* worth pursuing, sex involves the five "Ws" and the "H". Who, what, when, where, why, and how. By varying one or more of these factors, sex can be a little different from one time to the next. We'll take them in a slightly different order than usual:

"Where": The bedroom is not the only place in the house where privacy can be found. When the cat's away, the mice play. When the kids are away, the entire house is fair game. When the kids aren't away and aren't yet asleep, the closet in the master bedroom affords privacy and additional soundproofing. For those of us lucky enough to have a couple-only weekend away on occasion, a nice hotel room can be very inspiring.

"When": Weekdays are not off limits, as long as your kids are old enough to be unsupervised for a little while. Most kids watch some TV in the afternoon or early evening, meaning they are distracted and occupied. Seize the opportunity! SpongeBob can be a pretty good babysitter for a short while. Not only does this allow you time to "do the deed," but it feels like you're getting away with something, which makes it all that much more fun.

"Why": The reason for having sex should not be because it is Saturday night at 8:37pm. Sex should have an objective other than just getting it done. First and foremost, the sexual connection is important for keeping the passion and relationship alive, but there are other benefits that come from staying sexually active. Sex is a great stress reliever, and when a couple is stressed out after a particularly tough day, *stress sex* can be even better than *make up sex*. Sex also offers a distraction, an escape from life's problems, perhaps from reality, even if only for a little while.

> *Sex offers a shared escape from life's problems, if only for a while.*

"How": We'll leave this mostly to the reader's imagination. But within each individual's boundaries of propriety, sensibility,

religious beliefs, and comfort (both physical and moral) feel free to experiment and be adventurous, perhaps even creative. Communicate with one another without being judgmental or offended, while also being receptive and sensitive to the other person's boundaries.

"What": Sex is more than just intercourse and these non-intercourse activities are just as important to the relationship. Here are some examples:

- Caressing in bed, even if you aren't going to have intercourse
- Snuggling in the kitchen when the kids aren't looking
- Pulling your spouse in the pantry for a quick kiss and rub before resuming dinner preparations
- Playfulness is something that most new relationships have. Hold onto – or rekindle – the playfulness that your own relationship likely had when it was new but may have faded over the years

"Who": This one should be obvious, but there's certainly nothing wrong with making things interesting by doing some role playing.

When a person feels sexually happy and fulfilled at home, they have no need to stray. Keeping your sexual relationship interesting is the best way for both parties to have that fulfillment and keep them coming back for more.

Stoking the Fire of Marriage

Dating, sex, and intimacy are certainly some of the fun aspects of marriage, but what else can be done to keep the marriage fire alive? How much time one spends with one's spouse and what is done during that time has a significant impact on the relationship. Although this is common sense, many couples find themselves spending too much time apart, even on weekends, and not making the most of the precious little time they have together. Here are some pearls of wisdom for maximizing time together, both quantity and quality:

Take time to talk about why you love each other, and what it is that you love about each other. At the same time, remember that men and women are different. Women have much higher emotional intelligence than most men, and therefore it's much easier for them to have this type of emotional conversation. Men have to make up for shortcomings in the emotion area by having time to work through this emotionally heavy material. So, women, don't try to catch your man off-guard with this conversation. It will only have one possible result…hurt feelings. At the same time, you men out there need to be like Boy Scouts: always prepared. Think about these things regularly. It will prepare you for this conversation, and constantly remind you why you married this awesome person.

Make shared plans and goals for the future together, and keep revising and updating them as circumstances change. These goals might include buying a new house, vacation travel, starting a business together, a financial target, or anything else that can be a shared goal. Next, set aside time to pursue the goals together. This book is a good example of this concept. When we married, we had no idea we would be writing a book together. The writing of this book was a revision to our life goals as a couple, and this revision was made after we achieved many of our other goals in life. When this book is completed, we'll come up with another goal to accomplish together. Making, pursuing, and revising plans and goals is excellent material for conversation when the two of you are out on a date. But keep in mind the advice of author and futurist Joel A. Barker: vision without action is only a dream. It takes both vision and action to produce change, the result being achievement of your goals, and the ability to set the next goal.

> *It takes both vision and action to produce change.*

Have shared priorities and values. Having shared plans and goals is important, but these must align with a set of shared priorities that is already in place. For example, if you have agreed early on that your children will be your number one priority, having a secondary shared goal that is financial in nature and requires two incomes will conflict with that first priority as soon as the discussion of using daycare enters the conversation. Priorities must be discussed at length and in detail, agreed upon, and written down, before plans can be made and goals set. Use extreme caution before you adjust priorities to fit goals. Priorities and values should be chiseled into stone, goals should be written with ink, and plans should be written with a pencil.

It is important to each individual's character and well-being to **have individual hobbies and interests.** After all, a couple is made up of two individuals, and time together can only be appreciated more if time is spent apart. To the extent possible, those individual interests will augment, rather than replace, the couple's shared interests, and will provide a wellspring of outside information for conversation.

Shared interests are also very important to a strong relationship, and a primary source of conversation for a couple. While having common goals, as outlined above, can help to realign long-term shared vision, you must also have more immediate shared common interests to enable bonding on a regular basis. We're talking about things such as books, movies, hobbies, shopping, or anything else that you both enjoy and can talk about together, even if you aren't doing those activities together. If you've run out of common interests, find new ones! You can both take up skydiving, tennis, chess, camping, writing, or any number of other endeavors. Remember that most men are not ready to take up flower arranging, just as most women may not be willing to become college football enthusiasts. Compromises will have to be made on both sides, but there is an infinite number of hobbies and interests at your disposal.

While individual interests and hobbies are important, **avoid regular activities that pull you apart for very long periods of time.** If unavoidable, compensate and compromise in other areas. For example, if a husband knows that football season will have him watching football all day every Sunday with the guys, he needs to offset that time with family time/couple time on

Saturday. That is, during football season, don't spend every Saturday morning playing golf for four hours, and then work in the yard that whole afternoon, unless one or both of those are family bonding activities enjoyed by all. For the ladies, don't wait for Saturday to schedule your manicure, massage, and book club with the ladies, knowing full well most Sundays may be taken by worship, housework, and the frequent kids' birthday parties.

Celebrate victories, large and small. Birthdays and anniversaries only come around once a year and making a fuss about your spouse needs to happen more often than that, so look for every opportunity to do so. Some are obvious, such as job promotions, significant achievements in education, or the purchase or sale of a home. Less obvious opportunities for celebration include things such as achieving shared goals, reaching milestones in the raising of your children, or just finishing a large project around the house. What event is being celebrated, or precisely how it is being celebrated, is less important than the act of showing appreciation for one another and giving each other a pat on the back. Make cupcakes, go out for dinner, or just open a bottle of wine on a weeknight, but also take this chance to tell your spouse some of the qualities he or she possesses that you value and that enabled this achievement to happen.

Keep Fanning the Flames

If you're reading this book, there must be at least a spark left in your relationship. Some of the ideas suggested in this chapter may be just what is needed to fan that spark into flames. While predictability and safety are qualities that give stability to a mature relationship, it is spontaneity and passion that keep marriage *alive*.

The ideas expressed in this chapter, as well as the entire book, do not comprise an instruction manual. You know your spouse better than anyone else in the world, so if you know what buttons to push to make that person feel good, physically or emotionally, push them. Take every opportunity to fan the flames.

Happy is the man who finds a true
friend, and far happier is he who finds
that true friend in his wife.
- Franz Schubert

7

Happily Ever After I Do

Y ou've done it! Not only is the proverbial *seven-year itch* merely a distant memory, you've been happily married long enough for your fifteenth – or even twentieth – anniversary to be in your rearview mirror. Things are clicking, you and your spouse are making all the right moves, so it's nothing but smooth sailing from here. Right? That's entirely possible, but there's more to a successful lifelong marriage than just getting along with one another and making smart choices as they come at you. Decades-long success comes from making life plans and setting long-term goals as a couple, accomplishing those goals, then setting more.

Close your eyes and picture yourself and your spouse at a party celebrating your fiftieth wedding anniversary. You are surrounded by your children, grandchildren, possibly great-grandchildren, and other family and friends. A video will be shown with select footage from your fifty years of marriage. What do you hope will be included in the highlights of your married life? How can you make sure those highlights come to fruition, and what are you willing to do to make them come true? What sacrifices are you willing to make, and what risks are you willing to take?

Plans and goals are very personal, and no couple can dictate to another couple what the *right* goals are. In this chapter, we will highlight what we see as some of our own current goals to serve as examples. Your own goals must be specific and meaningful to you as a couple.

Never Stop Setting Goals

Look at your life as chapters in a book, with each chapter being a ten-year span. In chapter one you were born, and lived through your early childhood, and by the end of chapter two you have graduated from high school and started your college education or entered the working world. As you were living each chapter, you likely had images in your mind of all the great things you would accomplish in the next chapter, or even the one after that.

> *Don't let life interfere with being a couple.*

Looking back at the chapters that have gone by, how did the reality of them compare to the earlier visions? Some outcomes probably happened the way you thought they would, but there were almost certainly some major surprises and detours. Now, looking ahead at the chapters to come, you have images of what those years will look like. How do you ensure that those images stay on track and come to pass, even in the face of surprises?

Perhaps the first goal – and the one on which all other goals depend – is to never stop being a couple. That is, don't let parenthood, and the hustle and bustle of outside life, let you drift apart as husband and wife. It *is* possible to participate in the world, be good parents, and be a good couple at the same time; it just takes some work and planning, as already discussed in earlier chapters of this book.

Depending on where you are in your marriage, perhaps you feel as though you've already climbed the mountain of success and reached the summit. You've achieved financial security, perhaps your children have finished their education and are living a self-sufficient life, and your retirement savings is nearly complete. It would be easy to coast down the other side of that mountain, but this is a time to explore new goals for the next chapters of your life. Those goals will be very different from the ones that brought you to where you are today, and more than ever, with retirement on the horizon and the nest empty, those new goals will be entirely shared by husband and wife.

Over many years, and many cups of coffee and glasses of wine, we have constructed a list of goals for us to pursue as our children have been making those gradual steps toward adulthood and financial independence. Those goals include:

- Make new friends who are in a similar place in their life and with similar interests
- Work down our "bucket list" of travel destinations
- Travel with other couples that we enjoy being with
- Focus on health & fitness with a specific target in mind
- Pick up new hobbies, or actively pursue dormant ones
- Write and publish a book together :)

- Continue to learn through classes and self-education
- Explore new business ventures
- Find new volunteer activities to give back to the community

The key here is to choose goals that are meaningful and desirable to both you and your spouse, and pursue those goals together. Don't be afraid to make changes to the list when it makes sense to do so. At the same time, as mentioned earlier in the book, it's healthy to also pursue individual goals and activities, since personal happiness improves your life as a couple, and individual pursuits provide outside material for conversation and sharing.

Be Okay with Being Comfortable

Valentine's Day rolls around every February 14th, and this year is no different, coming up in just a couple days. Jack and Jill usually go out to a special dinner to celebrate the occasion, and are in the process of deciding which restaurant will get their money this year. With twenty-three years of marriage under their belts, Joey off to college, and Jimmy dividing his time between after-school activities and a girlfriend, the days of competing for a babysitter with every other married couple in the neighborhood are thankfully far behind them. So, it's just a matter of picking the perfect place to dine.

"How about that fish place over on Lexington?" Jill offers.

"Didn't we go there last month for Martin's birthday?" Jack replies.

"Yeah, that's right. Too soon."

"There's that Mexican place you like, with those amazing

enchiladas verdes." Jack says.

"That might be good, though the margaritas gave me a headache last time," Jill says.

"Ooh, that's right. And enchiladas without a margarita just doesn't seem right. Kinda sacrilegious."

"We could just pick something up and eat it here this year. Maybe some good Chinese takeout!" Jill says.

"Hmmm, interesting. You're sure you don't mind that for Valentine's Day?"

"Not at all. We can even make it romantic by dressing up a little, lighting some candles, set a nice table, you know, do it up right." Jill says.

"That is sounding better and better."

They both think in silence for a few minutes.

"Or," Jack says, "I can pick up a couple steaks and lobster tails and cook them right here in our kitchen."

"The weather's supposed to be sort of yucky on Valentine's Day, anyway, so that's a great idea."

"All right, all right, this is really starting to take shape!" Jack says. After a moment of pondering he adds, "you mentioned something about dressing up, but if we're not going anywhere, do we really want to dirty up our nice clothes?"

"I'm so glad you said that! As soon as those words left my mouth, I was thinking about how comfortable it would be to relax in my pajamas and enjoy the evening in comfort," Jill says.

"Now you're talkin'! I mean, we can still have the candles and all," he quickly adds, "but just do it in our pajamas. That's still romantic, right?"

"Or, we can just eat it in front of the television and watch a nice romantic comedy," Jill says.

Jack just looks at her and smiles, then takes her in his arms. "There's nothing in this universe I enjoy more than our quiet evenings at home. I can't think of a better way to celebrate Valentine's Day."

"Me, too," Jill says. "I love you."

"I love you, too," Jack says, kissing her.

Remember that feeling you had the first time you saw your spouse? How about the way you felt on your first night together? The passion, the mystery of discovery, the anticipation. Every time you parted ways you couldn't wait to see each other again. Wouldn't it be wonderful to be able to feel that way forever? But the reality is that it would be utterly exhausting. No relationship can maintain that level of fervor indefinitely, and a couple that believes it's possible will ultimately be disappointed, at least in that regard. Just as people change with time and maturity, so do relationships. The key is not to mistake relationship maturity for relationship deterioration.

When you buy a new pair of jeans, you buy them for the way they look and how they fit. With time, they will fade, perhaps get some holes in them, and just become more and more comfortable, to the point that you wish you could wear them all the time. They're not going to win any fashion shows, but you don't care; they're comfortable! A relationship can mature in the same way. It can get more comfortable with every passing year, comfortable in a good way. Comfortable in a way that makes you want to have that relationship wrapped

> *A comfortable, mature relationship is a goal, not a failing.*

around you all the time.

Some people may have a hard time using the word *comfortable* when describing happy marriage. In fact, if ten couples are asked to define what *happily married* means, they will likely give ten different answers, and they could all be right. There are many ways to achieve that lofty goal, but some couples, or just one spouse in the couple, may have an unrealistic expectation for *happily married*. They may expect romantic, candlelit meals at fancy restaurants daily, sexy pajamas in the dead of winter, gifts every Friday, and mindreading (as in "I shouldn't have to tell you"). But the realities of what makes for *happily married* are more grounded. There isn't an exact recipe, but some of the ingredients certainly include:

- Complete transparency
- Total honesty
- Open, respectful communication
- Knowing when to say sorry
- Doing things for the other person without being asked
- Seeing compromise as a gift to the other person
- Knowing – and feeling – that you can completely rely on the other person in good times and bad, and ensuring your spouse feels the same way through your own actions
- Finding ways to enjoy time together, and spending more of your free time with each other than you do with anyone else

Sure, the mushy romance stuff is good, and has its place, but there's nothing wrong – and everything right – about entering that comfortable stage of marriage that is more about interaction between man and wife, and less about exercising your credit card. Besides, giving your wife flowers might come in the form of holding her and telling her everything will be okay in a time of crisis. "Whispering sweet nothings" to your husband might simply be the act of making him a cup of coffee in the morning.

After three decades of marriage, though we still enjoy going out for dinner, whether just the two of us or with friends, some of our favorite moments as a couple involve curling up on the couch in our pajamas to watch our favorite television shows together. In fact, we have designated a specific daily "pajama time" so that we exercise at least a modicum of self-discipline and don't jump straight into pajamas the moment we get off from work. But make no mistake; this is couple time. When one of us is unavailable in the evening due to an external commitment, the other doesn't feel the *pajama pull*, because it is that shared comfortable time that makes it so enjoyable. What is your "pajama time"?

A Nest Gone Empty

If you already have a child, you know the impact that bringing this new being into your home can have. It is a truly life-changing event, and one where it is immediately clear that nothing will ever be the same again. An incredible amount of planning, coordination, and cooperation are needed by both parents to get through this period of transformation, from pregnancy to high school graduation. But, if you think the story ends there, or that life gets simpler when your chicks have flown, you're wrong. Transitioning to an empty nest can have just as many trials and tribulations, and this transition needs significant planning, coordination, and cooperation.

Many married couples struggle due to the change that comes with an empty nest. Empty Nest Syndrome affects a large percentage of parents, affecting both mothers and fathers. The most notable symptoms of ENS are sadness and feeling a loss of purpose, but it can also manifest itself in a parent who tries to maintain the same level of influ-

> *The empty nest is challenging; a married couple must reemerge.*

ence over their child even after that child has moved out. There are sociological indicators that you may be experiencing ENS, and overstepping boundaries with your adult offspring, such as:

- **Stalking them on social media:** They may not appreciate your "comments" as much as you think they do

- **Dropping in unannounced:** We all know why you're really there; and no, they will not keep their apartment as clean as you hope

- **Participating in their social activities:** Your child needs time with friends, as well as space from parents, in order to continue to grow as a person

- **Neglecting your spouse due to involvement with the adult child:** While you're doing the things listed above, how is your spouse spending his or her time?

The empty nest is your chance to spend quality time together as a couple, without feeling as though you're neglecting your children, with them now on their path to blissful independence. The empty nest also means that the whirlwind of activities that comes with being the parents of a minor child has come to an end. How are you going to use all that extra time? When the first child is born, a couple becomes a family, and when the last child leaves the nest, a couple reemerges. At the same time, it's still vitally important to maintain family interactions with your adult children through family dinners, vacations, and holiday traditions, to the extent possible, though those interactions look very different as your parenting evolves to more of an advisor, consultant, and sounding-board role.

In previous chapters we've discussed many ways for a couple to maintain a close, strong relationship, and those methods can certainly lessen the blow that comes with the suddenly empty nest. But there are a few more approaches that need to be considered that are specific to this life transition. In an earlier chapter, we discussed the importance of *date nights* to keep a couple feeling like a couple, despite the distractions of life. Ideally, you have been making time for this important activity since your first child was born, but as your youngest child begins driving, that is your signal to gradually accelerate the time dedicated to the transition from the full nest back to being a couple; when this is done right, it can feel like being newlyweds again. By starting – or accelerating – these activities prior to your last fledgling's move to the university dorm, the transition to the empty nest can be less traumatic.

Preparation for the empty nest – and avoidance of ENS – may fall more heavily on one parent than the other. That is, the empty nest will likely have a harder impact on a stay-home parent, and the high school years may be a time to begin looking for alternative projects or opportunities, such as returning to the workforce, volunteer activities, or hobbies that you've been waiting to pursue. Additionally, your child's newfound freedom that comes with a government issued driver's license should result in a reduction in soccer practice transportation for you, and that free time can be put to good use getting reacquainted with the person you've been married to all these years.

Speaking of new activities and new areas of focus, remember that business plan for your marriage and life? When your youngsters hit those high school years, that is the perfect time to review and update the plan. Not only do the post-high school years pose new financial challenges, your business plan should also be updated with the changes you plan to make to counter Empty Nest Syndrome.

The Best Years of Your Life

With the right planning, decision-making, and attitude, the second twenty years of marriage can be just as good – or even better – than the first twenty. The wisdom, financial security, and empty-nest freedom that can come with a mature marriage is what makes this possible. While this book cannot necessarily influence your attitude, the ideas and suggestions in this chapter, as well as many of the concepts described in earlier chapters, can help you with some of the planning and decision-making that is needed to help ensure lifelong marital happiness. It is in your hands.

There is nothing nobler or more
admirable than when two people who
see eye to eye keep house as man and
wife, confounding their enemies and
delighting their friends.
- Homer, *The Odyssey*

8

Epilogue: I Still Do

Jack and Jill went up the hill, still without a pail and no water in sight, but rather, to renew their vows of marriage after thirty-five amazing years. Their two grown sons are there to share the duty of "giving the bride away," and family and friends are gathered around to witness the event. Being married for that long is not a miracle; but being *happily* married for more than three decades is something special. The people present aren't surprised by this milestone, though they still may struggle to understand exactly how Jack and Jill's relationship works, and how it got to where it is.

Those same friends and family, when discussing Jack and Jill's marriage amongst themselves, have many theories for how it came to be. "They just got lucky." Or "You can't learn to have that kind of relationship; it has to come natural." Or "I don't believe they're really as happy as they seem to be." Or simply "They're weird," because it's easy to dismiss what one doesn't understand. But over the years when a single friend or family member has been looking for a potential soulmate, those same naysayers are the ones that have asked Jack and Jill time and again if they have a single brother or sister that they're hiding away somewhere, hoping whatever it is that creates that kind of relationship, it might run in the blood.

Certainly, personality and character play a part, but it is mostly the hundreds of little decisions, choices, and compromises Jack and Jill made every day that formed the foundation for their strong marriage. Those days quickly linked together to form weeks, months, and years, and before they knew it, they were celebrating their thirty-fifth anniversary. Any behavior that is done every day can become a habit, and they hope that their continuing habits as a married couple, through example, will inspire their sons, now fine young men, to find the same qualities in their own relationships.

There's no single answer, method, or *trick* to happy marriage. Every couple is different than every other couple in some way, and that makes life interesting. The concepts in this book must be adapted to the personality of the couple.

But one attribute that every couple needs for success is the desire and commitment to having the best possible relationship, prioritizing it above almost all other things. Like all worthwhile endeavors, marriage takes work and effort, and you must be willing to put in the time. Ask yourself each and every day, "What am I willing to do today to have a great relationship?" Whatever the answer is, go do it.

ABOUT THE AUTHORS

Estrella and Robert Cudmore have been married for more than thirty years. They have two sons, Dorian and Alec, and live in Austin, Texas.

Estrella was born and raised through her teen years in Cuernavaca, Mexico. She relocated to the United States with her family of origin at the age of sixteen, experiencing various parts of the country before settling in Texas. Estrella is a Certified Professional Coach, working with couples and individuals to achieve their life goals. With her coaching practice, Loran Coaching, she specializes in working with people facing life transitions, including marriage, first child, empty nest, and retirement.

Robert was born in Iowa but grew up in Southern California. He moved to Texas for a job opportunity and has called Austin home ever since. He is a Consultant and Business Coach specializing in sales and marketing strategy, where he can put his skills in the areas of logic, analysis, and operations to work to help clients achieve advanced data-driven decision-making. He also puts those skills to work as a Financial Coach working with retirees and soon-to-be-retirees to map out an effective retirement strategy.

Together, Estrella and Robert have spent many years working with engaged couples preparing for marriage, both through church ministry and through their coaching practice. Additionally, since it's never too late to have a great marriage, they also work with married couples who are looking to take their relationship from good to great.

www.LoranCoaching.com

Made in the USA
Coppell, TX
09 June 2021

57164599R00100